Visual Science Encyclopedia

Elements

▲ Sulfur is one of the few elements that is sufficiently unreactive to occur in its native state uncombined with other elements. It appears in yellow or amber translucent crystals.

How to use this book

Every word defined in this book can be found in alphabetical order on pages 3 to 47. There is also a full index on page 48. A number of other features will help you get the most out of the *Visual Science Encyclopedia*. They are shown below.

Here you will find the first word defined on any left-hand page.

Here you will find the last word defined on any right-hand page.

Each word is shown in bold so it is easy to find.

Each new letter of the alphabet is clearly marked to help you find the word you are looking for quicker.

Other words defined in the book are highlighted in bold.

Plus, many entries point to related words of interest.

Illustrations for some words complement the text and provide further information on a topic.

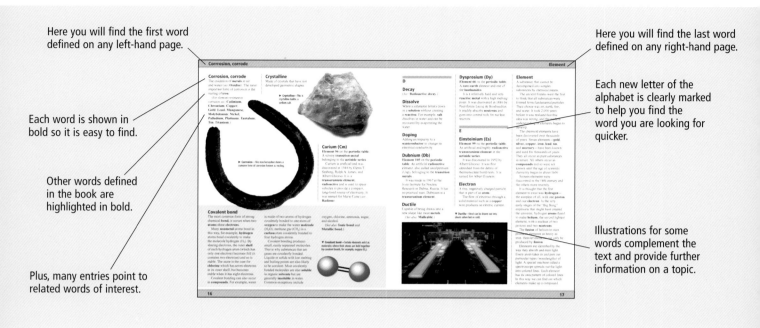

Acknowledgments

Grolier Educational

First published in the United States in 2002 by Grolier Educational, Sherman Turnpike, Danbury, CT 06816

Copyright © 2002 Atlantic Europe Publishing Company Ltd.

All rights reserved. No part of this publication may be reproduced, stored in a retrieval system, or transmitted in any form or by any means—electronic, mechanical, photocopying, recording, or otherwise—without prior permission of the publisher.

Author
Brian Knapp, BSc, PhD

Art Director
Duncan McCrae, BSc

Senior Designer
Adele Humphries, BA, PGCE

Editors
Lisa Magloff, BA, and Mary Sanders, BSc

Illustrations
David Woodroffe

Designed and produced by
EARTHSCAPE EDITIONS

Reproduced in Malaysia by
Global Color

Printed in Hong Kong by
Wing King Tong Company Ltd.

Library of Congress Cataloging-in-Publication Data
Visual Science Encyclopedia
    p. cm.
    Includes indexes.
    Contents: v. 1. Weather—v. 2.
Elements—v. 3. Rocks, minerals, and soil—
v. 4. Forces—v. 5. Light and sound—
v. 6. Water—v. 7. Plants—v. 8. Electricity
and magnetism—v. 9. Earth and space—
v. 10. Computers and the Internet—v. 11.
Earthquakes and volcanoes—v. 12. Heat
and energy.
    ISBN 0-7172-5595-6 (set: alk. paper)—ISBN
0-7172-5596-4 (v. 1: alk. paper)—ISBN
0-7172-5597-2 (v. 2: alk. paper)—ISBN
0-7172-5598-0 (v. 3: alk. paper)—ISBN
0-7172-5599-9 (v. 4: alk. paper)—ISBN
0-7172-5600-6 (v. 5: alk. paper)—ISBN
0-7172-5601-4 (v. 6: alk. paper)—ISBN
0-7172-5602-2 (v. 7: alk. paper)—ISBN
0-7172-5603-0 (v. 8: alk. paper)—ISBN
0-7172-5604-9 (v. 9: alk. paper)—ISBN
0-7172-5605-7 (v. 10: alk. paper)—ISBN
0-7172-5606-5 (v. 11: alk. paper)—ISBN
0-7172-5607-3 (v. 12: alk. paper)
    1. Science—Encyclopedias, Juvenile.
[1. Science—Encyclopedias.] I. Grolier
Educational (Firm)

QI21.V58 2001
503—dc21
                                    2001023704

Picture credits
All photographs are from the Earthscape Editions photolibrary.

This product is manufactured from sustainable managed forests. For every tree cut down, at least one more is planted.

A

Abundance of the elements

Element	% (in the universe)
Hydrogen	87
Helium	12
Oxygen	0.06
Carbon	0.03
Neon	0.02
Nitrogen	0.008
Silicon	0.003
Iron	0.002
Sulfur	0.002
Argon	0.0004
Magnesium	0.0003
Aluminum	0.0002
Calcium	0.0001
Sodium	0.0001
Phosphorus	0.00003
Potassium	0.000007

Actinide

An **element** belonging to the actinide **series**—15 similar **radioactive** elements running from **actinium** (**atomic number** 89) and **lawrencium** (atomic number 103) in **period 7** on the **periodic table**. The actinides are **transition metals**. The most well-known members of the series are **uranium** and **plutonium**, which are used in nuclear reactors to produce electrical energy.

All of the elements in the **group** are radioactive, and those from **americium** (atomic number 95) onward are made artificially in the laboratory and don't appear in nature.

Actinium (Ac)

Element 89 on the **periodic table**. A **radioactive** chemical element belonging to the **actinide series**.

It was discovered in 1899 by André-Louis Debierne. This rare, silvery-white **metal** glows blue in the dark. Actinium is one of the decay products of **uranium** (*see:* **Radioactive decay**).

Alchemy

A medieval practice of trying to turn certain "imperfect" **metals**, such as **lead**, into "perfect" metals, such as **gold**. This was called transmutation, and ways of doing it were shrouded in secrecy. Of course, the practice did not work, and alchemy gave way to scientific chemistry in the 18th century.

Alkali metals

The **elements** in **group 1** on the **periodic table**.

They are **lithium (Li)**, **sodium (Na)**, **potassium (K)**, **rubidium (Rb)**, **cesium (Cs)**, and **francium (Fr)**.

The alkali metals have a silvery luster. They can easily be made into new shapes (are **ductile**), and they conduct electricity and heat well. They have low melting points.

All of them are extremely **reactive** and interact violently with water. Most common nonmetallic substances (**nonmetals**) react with the alkali metals.

Alkaline-earth metals

The **elements** in **group 2** on the **periodic table**.

They are **beryllium (Be)**, **magnesium (Mg)**, **calcium (Ca)**, **strontium (Sr)**, **barium (Ba)**, and **radium (Ra)**. The term "alkaline-earths" comes from the fact that metal **oxides** are **soluble** in water and cannot be burned. They were traditionally called "earths." The "earths" that have properties similar to alkalis (soda ash and potash) were thus called alkaline earths. Quicklime (calcium oxide) is a common example.

▼▶ **Alkali metals**—Sodium is the most important alkali metal. It is highly reactive in air and even reacts under water. This is a piece of sodium metal in alcohol. Notice how it tarnishes as soon as it is cut. These pictures were taken about 30 seconds apart.

Aluminum conductor

Alloy

A mixture of two or more **elements**. Alloys are commonly mixtures of **metals**. For example, stainless steel contains **iron** and **chromium**, **bronze** mixes **copper** and **tin**, and **brass** is an alloy of copper and **zinc**. (*See also:* **Amalgam**.)

(*For other alloys see:* **Antimony**; **Beryllium**; **Bismuth**; **Cadmium**; **Cerium**; **Chromium**; **Cobalt**; **Gold**; **Hafnium**; **Iridium**; **Lead**; **Lithium**; **Magnesium**; **Molybdenum**; **Nickel**; **Niobium**; **Praseodymium**; **Rhodium**; **Ruthenium**; **Silver**; **Thorium**; **Tin**; **Titanium**.)

▲ **Alloy**—An alloy is a mixture of metals. This is solder, an alloy of tin and lead.

◄ **Aluminum**—Aluminum is a good electrical conductor and widely used for carrying power supplies from power plants to local areas.

Sodium hydroxide

Aluminum

Element 13 on the **periodic table**. A lightweight, silvery-white **metal**. It belongs to **group 3** (the **boron group**).

Aluminum is the most common metallic element in the Earth's crust. It is the third most abundant element on Earth after **oxygen** and **silicon** and makes up about 8% by weight of the Earth's crust.

Aluminum is **reactive** and is only found naturally as aluminum **oxide**. Corundum (emery) is made of crystals of aluminum oxide and is mined as a natural abrasive. Other aluminum oxide crystals include rubies and sapphires.

The mined ore of aluminum is called bauxite.

Named by Sir Humphry Davy in 1809, aluminum is difficult to separate from its oxide. It was first separated by Hans Christian Ørsted only in 1825.

It was so difficult to obtain that it was very expensive and used as a **precious metal**. But when electric power became available, it could be more easily refined, and the price dropped. At the same time, it found many new uses.

Aluminum is now the most widely used **nonferrous** metal.

◄ **Aluminum**—Aluminum reacts with alkalis as well as acids. This is what happens when sodium hydroxide is placed in an aluminum pie plate.

Amalgam

A liquid **alloy** of **mercury** and another **metal** or metals.

Americium (Am)

Element 95 on the **periodic table**. An artificial, silvery-white, and highly **radioactive metal** in the **actinide** series.

It is also called a **transuranium element** because it has a higher **atomic mass** than **uranium**. It is made from **plutonium** in a nuclear reactor.

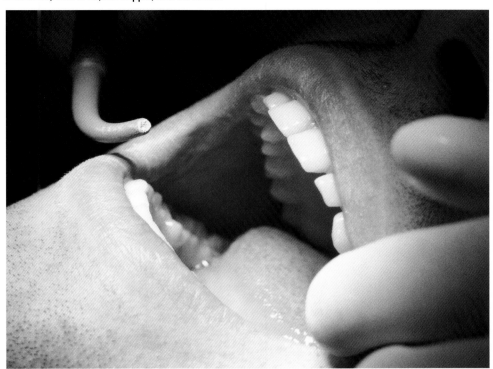

▼ **Amalgam**—Dental amalgam is an alloy of 52% mercury, 33% silver, 12.5% tin, 2% copper, and 0.5% zinc.

▲ **Americium**—Americium is a radioactive source used in smoke detectors.

Anion

A negatively charged **ion**.

Antimony (Sb)

Element 51 on the **periodic table**. A **metalloid** in **group 5** (the **nitrogen group**) that gets its symbol from its Latin name *stibium*.

It is a silvery, bluish-white solid that is very brittle and has a flaky texture. It is found as a gray sulfide **mineral** called stibnite. Antimony is a poor conductor of heat and electricity. It **tarnishes** only slightly in air, more in moist air. When heated in air, it burns with a brilliant blue flame. It has no uses as a pure metal; but when alloyed with other metals, it makes the **alloy** hard and strong. **Compounds** of antimony are used to make materials flame-proof and as paint colorings.

Argon (Ar)

Element 18 on the **periodic table**. An **inert** (unreactive) gas and the most abundant member of **group 8** (the **noble gases**).

It is colorless, odorless, and tasteless. It was isolated in 1894, from air, by British scientists Lord Rayleigh and Sir William Ramsay.

Argon makes up about 1.3% of the atmosphere by weight and 0.94% by volume. When electricity passes through argon, it glows pale red. It is used in light bulbs and other places where an unreactive gas is needed, for example, in the manufacture of **silicon** chips.

▲ **Argon**—Argon is the gas used in many light bulbs.

Arsenic (As)

Element 33 on the **periodic table**. A chemical element in **group 5** (the **nitrogen group**).

It is a **nonmetal** common in nature as **compounds** and occasionally in gray and yellow elemental form. Gray arsenic is very brittle and **tarnishes** in air; the yellow form is softer. Arsenic sublimes—changing from solid to vapor and back to solid again without becoming a liquid in between. Arsenic is well known as a poison. Arsenic **oxide** is used as a pesticide, in adhesives, and as a decolorizer in glassmaking. It is also used in the **doping** of **silicon** in integrated circuit making.

Astatine (At)

Element 85 on the **periodic table**. A **radioactive halogen** element and the heaviest member of **group 7** (the halogens). It is a **metalloid**, is unstable, and has no practical uses.

Atom

The smallest particle of an **element**.

The ancient Greek philosopher Democritus thought that all matter was made of atoms of what the Greeks believed to be the four elements—earth, air, fire, and water. Later, it was discovered that atoms are made of even smaller particles called **protons**, **neutrons**, and **electrons**. Neutrons and protons are found in the core of the atom, called the nucleus, which contains nearly all of the mass of the atom. The total number of protons and neutrons is called the **atomic mass**. The number of protons in the nucleus gives the **atomic number** of the element, and it also equals the number of electrons in the atom.

The chemical characteristics of elements depend on the number of electrons, and on the way in which the atoms are arranged.

Because of this, elements can be distinguished from each other by their atomic numbers.

(*See also:* **Fission**; **Fusion**; **Ion**; **Isotopes**; **Molecule**.)

Atomic mass

The mass of an **atom** measured in atomic mass units (amu). One atomic mass unit equals the mass of one-twelfth of the atom of carbon-12 (*see:* **Carbon** and **Isotope**). Atomic mass is now used more generally than atomic weight. The atomic mass of **chlorine**, for example, is about 35 amu.

(*See also:* **Relative atomic mass**.)

Atomic number

The number of **electrons** or the number of **protons** in an **atom**. Also known as proton number. For example, the atomic number for **gold** is 79 and for **carbon** is 6. Used commonly to describe the element number on the **periodic table** (for example, element 79 for gold and element 6 for carbon).

Atomic weight

(*See:* **Atomic mass**.)

B

Barium (Ba)

Element 56 on the **periodic table**. One of the **group 2** elements (**alkaline-earth metals**).

It is silvery-white when freshly cut and slightly heavier than **lead**. It is mainly found as the **mineral** barite. This element is used in metallurgy, and its **compounds** are used in fireworks, petroleum mining, and radiology.

Barium sulfate is used as a white filler in rubber and paper. It is also

▼ **Atom**—The diagrams below represent atoms of the elements carbon and gold. The total number of electrons is shown in the relevant shells around the central nucleus.

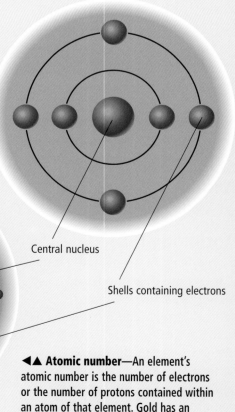

An atom of carbon

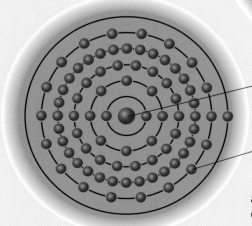

An atom of gold

Central nucleus

Shells containing electrons

◄▲ **Atomic number**—An element's atomic number is the number of electrons or the number of protons contained within an atom of that element. Gold has an atomic number of 79 and carbon 6.

a tracer in medicine (X-rays can trace a "barium meal"). It also helps make a brilliant white coloring substance for paint. Barium nitrate produces the green color in signal flares and in fireworks.

Berkelium (Bk)

Element 97 on the **periodic table**. An artificial element in the **actinide series**. It was discovered in 1949 by Stanley Thompson, Albert Ghiorso, and Glenn Seaborg when they bombarded **americium** with **helium ions**. It is named after the University of California at Berkeley. All of the **isotopes** of berkelium are **radioactive**. No one has ever seen metallic berkelium, but it is expected to be a silvery **metal** similar to others in the actinide series.

Beryllium (Be)

Element 4 on the **periodic table**. Beryllium is a brittle, steel-gray **metal**. It is one of the **alkaline-earth metals** (**group 2** elements).

It is found combined in nature in the **mineral** beryl. Beryllium in metal **alloys** adds hardness.

▲ **Bismuth**—Crystals of bismuth can be created artificially.

▲ **Beryllium**—The most common natural compound of beryllium is the mineral beryl (beryllium aluminum silicate).

Bismuth (Bi)

Element 83 on the **periodic table**. The most metallic of the elements in **group 5** (the **nitrogen group**).

Bismuth was first described in 1450 by the German monk Basil Valentine. Bismuth **compounds** were traditionally used for digestive problems and for skin ailments.

Bismuth is hard, brittle, and gray-white. It is used to make low melting point **alloys** and in solders and the triggers in automatic sprinkler heads.

Bohrium (Bh)

Element 107 on the **periodic table**. An artificial **radioactive** element, (also called unnilseptium—Uns), belonging to the **transition metals**.

It was discovered in 1976 at the Joint Institute for Nuclear Research in Dubna, Russia. It has no practical uses. Bohrium is a **transuranium element**.

Bond

The force that holds together **atoms** or **molecules**.

There are a number of types of bond, such as **covalent bonds**, **ionic bonds**, **metallic bonds**, and hydrogen bonds. Some are strong (covalent and ionic bonds), and some are weak (hydrogen bonds).

Chemical bonds form molecules because the linked particles are more stable than the unlinked particles. For example, the **hydrogen** molecule (H) is more stable than single atoms of hydrogen, so hydrogen gas is always found as two molecules of two bonded atoms.

(*See also:* **Valency**.)

Boron (B)

Element 5 on the **periodic table**. A **metalloid** of **group 3** (the **boron group**).

It is a very hard, black **semiconductor**. It will scratch corundum and can be used as an abrasive. Boron is commonly found in the **mineral** borax.

Boron was discovered in 1808 by French scientists Joseph-Louis Gay-Lussac and Louis-Jacques Thenard, and also by British scientist Sir Humphry Davy.

It is used to increase hardness in steel. Borosilicate glass is the common heat-proof glass used for ovenware, often under the trade name Pyrex®.

Boron group elements

The **elements** in **group 3** on the **periodic table**, which include **boron (B)**, **aluminum (Al)**, **gallium (Ga)**, **indium (In)**, and **thallium (Tl)**.

Boron is the lightest of the group and is a **metalloid**; all the others are silvery-white **metals**. In terms of usefulness aluminum is by far the most important member of the group.

Boyle, Robert

The English chemist Robert Boyle (1627-1691) was the first to understand that all matter was made of fundamental substances that could not be **reduced** by physical or chemical means—**elements**.

In 1661 he pointed out that the four Greek "elements" of earth, fire, air, and water could not be the real chemical elements because they cannot combine to form other substances, nor can they be extracted from other substances.

Brass

A **metal alloy** mainly of **copper** and **zinc**.

Bromine (Br)

Element 35 on the **periodic table**. One of the **halogens** (**group 7** elements).

It is an amber-brown gas that is highly poisonous. In 1826 the French chemist Antoine-Jérôme Balard discovered bromine as a **compound** in **salt** left after the evaporation of seawater. Bromine compounds (bromides) are used in photography and as sedatives in medicine.

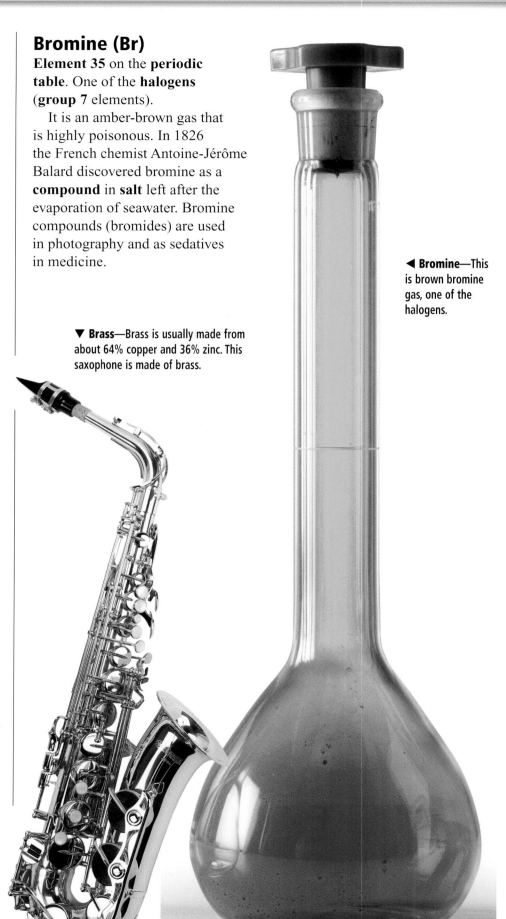

▼ **Brass**—Brass is usually made from about 64% copper and 36% zinc. This saxophone is made of brass.

◄ **Bromine**—This is brown bromine gas, one of the halogens.

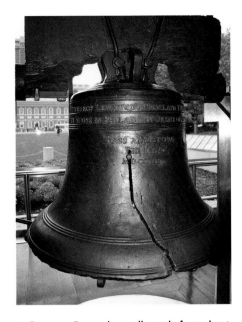

▲ **Bronze**—Bronze is usually made from about 78% copper and 12% tin. The less tin, the softer the metal will be, so usually no more than 28% tin is added. Bells are often made from bronze. This is the Liberty Bell in Philadelphia.

Bronze
An **alloy** mainly of **copper** and **tin**.

C

Cadmium (Cd)
Element 48 on the **periodic table**. A silvery-white **metal** and one of the **transition metals**.

Cadmium is a soft metal with a low melting point. Friedrich Stromeyer, a German chemist, discovered it in 1817.

Cadmium is used for electroplating steel, **iron**, **copper**, **brass**, and other **alloys** to protect them from **corrosion**. Because it absorbs **neutrons**, cadmium also goes into control rods in nuclear reactors.

Calcium (Ca)
Element 20 on the **periodic table**. A silvery **alkaline-earth metal** (**group 2** element).

First isolated by British scientist Sir Humphry Davy in 1808, it does not occur as a native **metal**, but in **compounds**, of which calcium carbonate (limestone) is the most common. Bones are made of calcium phosphate. As calcium oxide (lime), it goes into cement and as a fertilizer.

▼ **Calcium**—Calcium carbonate makes limestone rocks and the calcite that forms fossils and crystals.

◄ **Calcium**—Calcium metal quickly tarnishes in air.

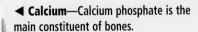

◄ **Calcium**—Calcium phosphate is the main constituent of bones.

Californium (Cf)
Element 98 on the **periodic table**. An artificial metallic **radioactive** element in the **actinide series**. It is a **transuranium element** and makes a very intense source of light in medicine.

Carbon (C)

Element 6 on the **periodic table**. A **nonmetallic** element in **group 4** (the **carbon group**).

Carbon is found in about 90% of all known **compounds**, even though it is not especially plentiful. The **isotope** carbon-12 is the standard relative to which the **atomic mass** of all the other elements is measured. The isotope carbon-14 is **radioactive** and is used for radiocarbon dating.

Carbon makes **crystalline** diamond and graphite as well as the deposit called carbon black. Diamond—the hardest natural substance—is a transparent gemstone and is a poor conductor of electricity. It is used as a cutting tool. Graphite is opaque, soft, and conducts electricity very well. Its slippery properties make it useful as a lubricant and as the "lead" in pencils.

Of the many noncrystalline forms of carbon, the most common are coal, coke, and charcoal. They are used as fuels. Charcoal can also filter gases, remove the color from materials, and go into gunpowder.

Carbon appears in all living matter.

▶ **Carbon**—The cutting down of trees has a major effect on the natural carbon cycle because it removes a natural carbon-absorbing part of the environment (called a carbon "sink"). To maintain balance in the carbon cycle, trees have to be replanted as they are felled. This is happening in the temperate lands, but not in the tropics.

Carbon group elements

Another term for the **group 4 elements** on the **periodic table**, which include **carbon (C)**, **silicon (Si)**, **germanium (Ge)**, **tin (Sn)**, and **lead (Pb)**.

◀ **Carbon**—Plants need carbon to make the cells of their bodies. They extract carbon from carbon dioxide gas, using the energy in sunlight.

▶ **Carbon**—This is the atomic structure of diamond. It is built of interlocking carbon atoms with no room for other atoms to form part of the structure. That is why diamonds are so hard.

◀ **Carbon**—This piece of Kimberlite rock shows the way that most diamond occurs, as a dull yellowish mineral set in a rock background.

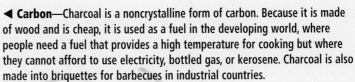

◄ **Carbon**—Charcoal is a noncrystalline form of carbon. Because it is made of wood and is cheap, it is used as a fuel in the developing world, where people need a fuel that provides a high temperature for cooking but where they cannot afford to use electricity, bottled gas, or kerosene. Charcoal is also made into briquettes for barbecues in industrial countries.

▼ **Carbon**—Crude oil contains hydrocarbons. From these hydrocarbons come the fuels that power the modern world, and the raw materials for plastics, fertilizers, and drugs.

▲ **Carbon**—Carbohydrate foods all contain carbon, hydrogen, and oxygen, and cover a wide range of natural compounds such as sugar and starch. Potatoes, pasta, and rice are typical carbohydrate foods.

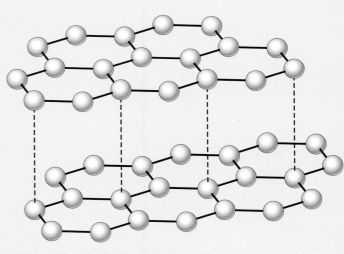

Graphite

▲▼ **Carbon**—This is the atomic structure of graphite. Like diamond, it is made only of carbon. Unlike diamond, however, the structure of graphite is in sheets. The bonds between the sheets are relatively weak, so that when pressure is applied, parts of the mineral flake off. That is what allows graphite to be used in pencils.

Catalyst

A substance that speeds up a chemical **reaction**, but itself remains unaltered at the end of the reaction.

(*See also:* **Cobalt**; **Palladium**; **Platinum**; **Transition elements**.)

Cation

A positively charged **ion**.

Cerium (Ce)

Element 58 on the **periodic table**. A **rare-earth metal** and one of the **lanthanides**. It is iron-gray and about as soft as **tin**.

Cerium was discovered in 1803 by Jöns Jacob Berzelius, Wilhelm Hisinger, and Martin Klaproth. It was named after the asteroid Ceres. Although cerium is not widely known, it is as common on Earth as **copper**.

It is used for fine polishing of glass, to make porcelain more

▼ **Catalyst**—The demonstration shown here uses the metal cobalt as a catalyst to speed up the breakdown of the chemical hydrogen peroxide. The reaction is so fast that, as oxygen is produced, it forms big bubbles that froth up the liquid so that the froth reaches nearly to the top of the glass tube. The reaction is over in a few seconds.

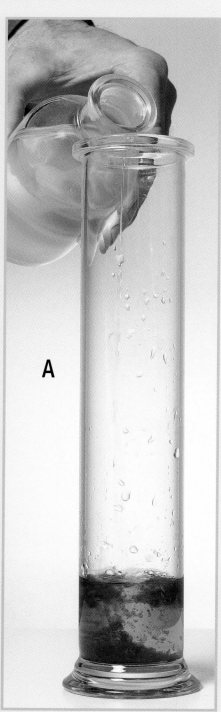

A

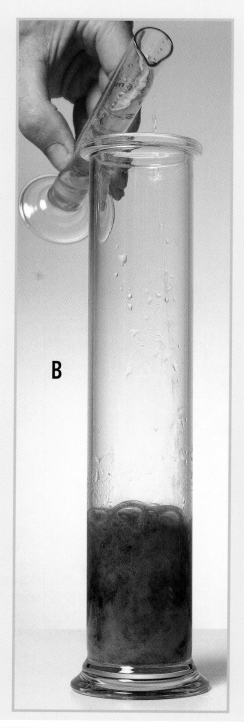

B

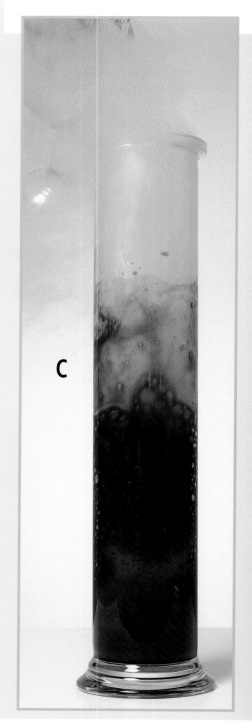

C

A chlorine (Cl) atom is released from CFCs and carried into the upper atmosphere by air currents.

Ozone (O₃) molecules are formed in the upper atmosphere.

Chlorine and ozone combine to produce chlorine oxide and oxygen (O₂).

The O₂ breaks down in oxygen (O) and reacts with chlorine oxide to produce an oxygen (O₂) molecule and a single chlorine atom.

This very reactive chlorine atom is called a "free radical." It can now react with another ozone molecule, causing further destruction of the ozone layer.

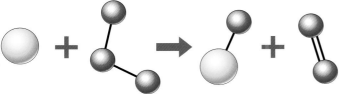

| Chlorine atom Cl | Ozone molecule O_3 | Chlorine oxide ClO | Oxygen molecule O_2 | Chlorine oxide ClO | Oxygen atom O | Oxygen molecule O_2 | Chlorine atom Cl |

▲ **Chlorine**—Chlorofluorocarbons (CFCs) have been widely used to make the coolant in refrigerators. CFCs include chlorine, fluorine, and carbon. When CFCs reach the stratosphere, they are broken down by ultraviolet solar radiation, releasing chlorine atoms. These atoms attack the ozone molecules. A single chlorine atom can survive in the stratosphere for four to ten years, and during that time it can destroy countless ozone molecules. CFC-free substitutes are now being produced.

opaque, and to clear color impurities from glass. It is also widely used as an alloying metal, for example, in jet engines, where it raises the melting point of the **alloy**.

Cesium (Cs)

Element 55 on the **periodic table**. A member of **group 1** (the **alkali metals**), it was discovered in 1860 by Robert Bunsen and Gustav Kirchhoff. It is a silvery-white alkali **metal** named from the Latin *caesius*, meaning "sky-blue" (its color when heated).

Cesium is an extremely soft metal that is liquid at room temperature. It reacts explosively with cold water and combines with **oxygen**. It also easily loses **electrons** when struck by light and is used for photoelectric cells. Cesium is also used in atomic clocks.

Chalcogen

Oxygen (O), **sulfur (S)**, **selenium (Se)**, and **tellurium (Te)** are the four chalcogens and are members of **group 6** (the **oxygen group**) on the **periodic table**.

The word comes from the Greek meaning "brass maker" because all these **elements** are found in **copper** ores, and copper is the most important **metal** in **brass** making.

Chlorine (Cl)

Element 17 on the **periodic table**. A greenish-yellow gas and the second lightest **halogen** (**group 7** element).

Chlorine is very **corrosive** and poisonous. It is heavier than air and **dissolves** in water.

Chlorine appears most commonly as the **compound** sodium chloride, common **salt**, and is part of hydrochloric acid.

Chlorine was discovered in 1774 by Carl Wilhelm Scheele but named by Sir Humphry Davy in 1810.

Chlorine can be used for bleaching and as a disinfectant in water supplies. It is also widely used in the manufacture of plastics such as PVC.

▶ **Chlorine**—Chlorine is a greenish-yellow gas.

▲ **Chromium**—A chromium-plated wheel.

Chromium (Cr)

Element 24 on the **periodic table**. A steel-gray **metal** and one of the **transition metals**.

It is very hard and can be polished. It resists **corrosion**, does not **tarnish** in air or corrode in water, and can be used in an **alloy** to increase hardness and to resist corrosion. Stainless steel is an alloy of **iron** and chromium.

Chromium was discovered in 1797 by the French chemist Nicolas-Louis Vauquelin.

Chromium **compounds** are highly colored. They give their color to many natural substances such as emerald and ruby.

Cobalt (Co)

Element 27 on the **periodic table**. One of the **transition metals**. Although the distinctive blue color of cobalt **compounds** had been used since ancient times, it was only in 1735 that the Swedish chemist Georg Brandt discovered its source to be the element cobalt.

Cobalt is also an essential part of blood cells as vitamin B_{12}.

Cobalt is a scarce **metal** usually found as a trace element among ores of other elements such as **iron** and **zinc**. It is normally recovered as a by-product of refining these metals. Cobalt is very **reactive**, and if finely divided, it will ignite spontaneously.

Cobalt is magnetic and has a high melting point, so it can be used where magnetism is required in a hot environment. **Radioactive isotopes** of cobalt are used for medical purposes and also to look for flaws in materials.

The main use of cobalt is as a metal in **alloys**, both for high temperature permanent magnets and for making very hard steels. Cobalt phosphate is a blue coloring agent in ceramics and glass.

(*See also:* **Catalyst**.)

Coinage metals

The **metals copper**, **gold**, and **silver**.

Combustion

A chemical **reaction** between **oxygen** and another substance. Some combustion reactions are slow, such as the combustion of the sugars we eat that provide energy for our bodies. If the combustion results in a flame, it is called burning.

Compound

A chemical consisting of two or more **elements** bonded together. (*See also:* **Bond**; **Covalent bond**; **Oxide**; **Reduce, reduction**; **Salt**.)

(*For more on compounds see:* **Antimony**; **Barium**; **Bismuth**; **Bromine**; **Calcium**; **Carbon**; **Chlorine**; **Chromium**; **Cobalt**; **Gallium**; **Hydrogen**; **Iodine**; **Iridium**; **Magnesium**; **Silicon**; **Sodium**; **Transition elements**; **Vanadium**.)

▼ **Combustion**—Combustion of steel in oxygen.

Copper (Cu)

Element 29 on the **periodic table**. A soft, easily bent **metal** belonging to the **transition metals**.

It is a very good conductor of electricity and heat. Copper occurs by itself as an orange metal called native copper.

Native copper was the first metal people made things from. Records of its use go back over 10,000 years, when it began to replace stone. About 5,500 years ago it was alloyed with **tin** to make **bronze**. The name copper is a form of the Roman name for Cyprus, the island where the ancient Romans got most of their copper.

Today copper mainly goes into electric cables and **alloys** with other metals to make bronze, **brass** (with **zinc**), or **nickel silver** (with zinc and nickel—no silver is used at all). It is also widely used for coins.

Copper does not **corrode** easily except to produce a thin green protective coat of copper carbonate. As a result, it can be a roofing material.

◀ **Copper**—This is native copper together with quartz crystals. Miners would call the quartz "gangue," meaning a material of no value that is mined together with the metal.

▼ **Copper**—Copper ores can be mined with as little as about one-half of 1% copper content. This picture from Arizona shows one of the world's most important copper mines.

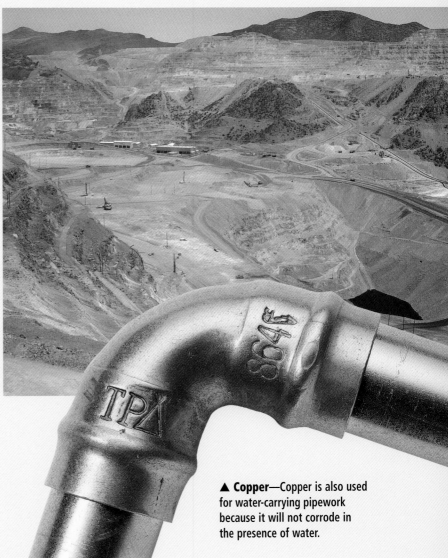

◀ **Copper**—Copper is used for the cladding on the Statue of Liberty because of both its attractive color and its longevity against corrosion.

▲ **Copper**—Copper is also used for water-carrying pipework because it will not corrode in the presence of water.

Corrosion, corrode

The oxidation of **metals** in air and water (*see*: **Oxidize**). The most important form of corrosion is the rusting of **iron**.

(*For elements resistant to corrosion see:* **Cadmium**; **Chromium**; **Copper**; **Gold**; **Lead**; **Manganese**; **Molybdenum**; **Nickel**; **Palladium**; **Platinum**; **Tantalum**; **Tin**; **Titanium**.)

Crystalline

Made of crystals that have not developed geometric shapes.

▶ **Crystalline**—This is crystalline halite, a sodium salt.

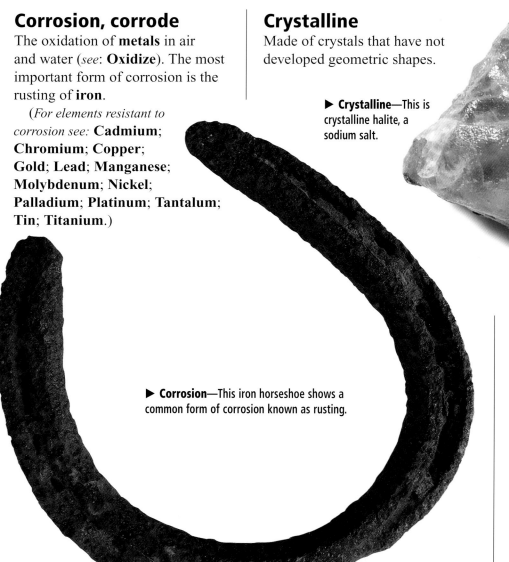

▶ **Corrosion**—This iron horseshoe shows a common form of corrosion known as rusting.

Curium (Cm)

Element 96 on the **periodic table**. A silvery **transition metal** belonging to the **actinide series**.

Curium is artificial and was discovered in 1944 by Glenn T. Seaborg, Ralph A. James, and Albert Ghiorso. It is a **transuranium element**, **radioactive** and is used in space vehicles to provide a compact, long-lived source of electricity. It was named for Marie Curie (*see:* **Radium**).

Covalent bond

The most common form of strong chemical **bond**, it occurs when two **atoms** share **electrons**.

Many **nonmetal** atoms bond in this way, for example, **hydrogen** atoms bond covalently to make the molecule hydrogen (H_2). By sharing electrons, the outer **shell** of each hydrogen atom (which has only one electron) becomes full (it contains two electrons) and so is stable. The same is the case for **chlorine**, which has seven electrons in its outer shell, but becomes stable when it has eight electrons.

Covalent bonding can also occur in **compounds**. For example, water is made of two atoms of hydrogen covalently bonded to one atom of **oxygen** to make the water **molecule** (H_2O); methane gas (CH_4) is a **carbon** atom covalently bonded to four hydrogen atoms.

Covalent bonding produces small, easily separated molecules. That is why substances that are gases are covalently bonded. Liquids or solids with low melting and boiling points are also likely to be covalent. Most covalently bonded molecules are also **soluble** in organic **solvents** but are generally **insoluble** in water. Common exceptions include oxygen, chlorine, ammonia, sugar, and alcohol.

(*See also:* **Ionic bond** and **Metallic bond**.)

▼ **Covalent bond**—Certain elements exist as molecules in which their atoms are held together by covalent bonds, for example, oxygen (O_2).

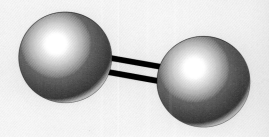

D

Decay
(*See:* **Radioactive decay**.)

Dissolve
When a substance breaks down in a **solution** without creating a **reaction**. For example, **salt** dissolves in water and can be recovered by evaporating the water.

Doping
Adding an impurity to a **semiconductor** to change its electrical conductivity.

Dubnium (Db)
Element 105 on the **periodic table**. An artificial **radioactive** element, also called unnilpentium (Unp), belonging to the **transition metals**.

It was made in 1967 at the Joint Institute for Nuclear Research in Dubna, Russia. It has no practical uses. Dubnium is a **transuranium element**.

Ductile
Capable of being drawn into a new shape like most **metals**.
(*See also:* **Malleable**.)

Dysprosium (Dy)
Element 66 on the **periodic table**. A **rare-earth** element and one of the **lanthanides**.

It is a relatively hard and very **reactive metal** with a high melting point. It was discovered in 1886 by Paul-Émile Lecoq de Boisbaudran. It readily absorbs **neutrons** and goes into control rods for nuclear reactors.

E

Einsteinium (Es)
Element 99 on the **periodic table**. An artificial and highly **radioactive transuranium element** in the **actinide series**.

It was discovered in 1952 by Albert Ghiorso. It was first identified from the debris of thermonuclear bomb tests. It is named for Albert Einstein.

Electron
A tiny, negatively charged particle that is part of an **atom**.

The flow of electrons through a solid material such as a **copper** wire produces an electric current.

▼ Ductile—Steel can be drawn out into sheets when hot or cold.

Element
A substance that cannot be decomposed into simpler substances by chemical means.

The ancient Greeks were the first to think that all substances were formed from fundamental particles. Their choice was air, earth, fire, and water. It took 2,000 years before it was realized that this idea was wrong, and the modern understanding of elements began to develop.

The chemical elements have been discovered over thousands of years. Seven elements—**gold**, **silver**, **copper**, **iron**, **lead**, **tin**, and **mercury**—have been known and used for thousands of years. They all occur as pure substances in nature. All others occur as **compounds** and so were not known until the age of scientific chemistry began in about 1600.

Sixteen elements were discovered in the 18th century and the others more recently.

It is thought that the first element to exist was **hydrogen**—the simplest of all, with one **proton** and one **electron**. In the very early stages of the "Big Bang" explosion that might have created the universe, hydrogen **atoms** fused to make **helium**, the second lightest element, with a nucleus of two protons and two **neutrons**.

The **fusion** of helium in stars produces elements as heavy as iron. Heavier elements can only be produced by **fission**.

Elements are identified by the way they absorb and emit light. Every atom takes in and puts out particular types (wavelengths) of light. A special machine called a spectroscope spreads out the light into colored lines. Each element has its own pattern of colored lines. In this way we can find out which elements make up a compound.

Elements, renaming

Since the 1950s new **elements** have been discovered in the United States, Germany, and Russia. However, no one agreed on what to call them. In part this was because people could not agree on who first discovered each element. The person who discovers a new element has the right to give it a name.

International committees to name elements have also not met with success. For example, they rejected the U.S. naming of element 106 as seaborgium for Nobel prize winner Glenn T. Seaborg. As a result, the American Chemical Society used a largely different group of names from those in other countries. This problem was resolved in 1997. As a result, the official names and symbols of elements 101 to 109 are: 101, **mendelevium (Md)**; 102, **nobelium (No)**; 103, **lawrencium (Lr)**; 104, **rutherfordium (Rf)**; 105, **dubnium (Db)**; 106, **seaborgium (Sg)**; 107, **bohrium (Bh)**; 108, **hassium (Hs)**; and 109, **meitnerium (Mt)**.

Emulsion

A suspension of one liquid in another. The suspension is in the form of droplets. In an emulsion the two liquids must not be able to mix (immiscible).

Erbium (Er)

Element 68. A grayish-silver **rare-earth metal** and one of the **lanthanides** on the **periodic table**.

Discovered in 1843 by Carl Gustaf Mosander, it is important in fiber-optic telecommunications.

Europium (Eu)

Element 63 on the **periodic table**. A **rare-earth metal** and one of the **lanthanides**, discovered in 1896 by Eugène-Anatole Demarçay.

F

Fermium (Fm)

Element 100 on the **periodic table**. An artificial and **radioactive** element of the **actinide series**. It is a **transuranium element**.

Fermium was discovered by Albert Ghiorso in 1952.

Fission

The breakdown of the structure of an **atom**.

Fission is popularly called "splitting the atom" because the atom is divided into approximately two other nuclei (singular is nucleus). It is different from, for example, the small change that happens when **radioactivity** is emitted.

▼ **Fission**—The chain reaction of uranium fission.

▶ **Fluorine**—Chains of units like the one shown below form solid polytetrafluoroethene. The fluorine atoms shield the carbon atoms that make the chain (polymer). Thus the carbon atoms form a polymer that is shielded from reaction by the fluorine: the secret of Teflon's® nonstick success.

Fluorine (F)

Element 9 on the **periodic table**. The lightest **halogen** (**group 7** element).

A pale yellow gas slightly heavier than air, fluorine is the most **reactive** chemical element. It combines with all other elements except **helium**, **neon**, and **argon**.

The French chemist Henri Moissan discovered fluorine in 1886.

It is mainly found as the **mineral** fluorite—calcium fluoride. It also appears in bones and teeth. Adding fluoride to water has become popular because it helps teeth resist decay.

Fluorine is an extremely poisonous gas.

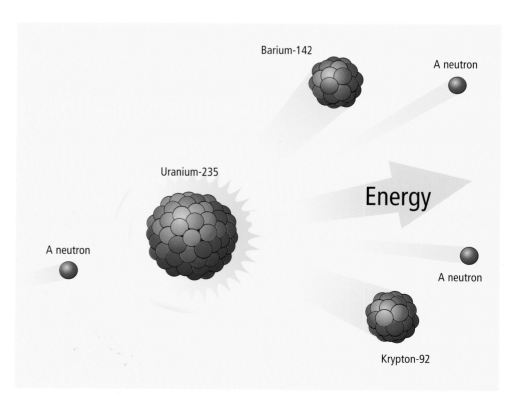

Barium-142

A neutron

Uranium-235

Energy

A neutron

A neutron

Krypton-92

Discovered by J. C. G. de Marignac and Paul-Émile Lecoq de Boisbaudran in 1880, gadolinium was named for the Finnish chemist Johan Gadolin. It is used in electronic components.

Gallium (Ga)

Element 31 on the **periodic table**. A rare silvery-white **metal** of the **boron group**, which is **group 3**.

It has a melting point just above room temperature. Gallium was discovered by Paul-Émile Lecoq de Boisbaudran in 1875 as an impurity in zinc blende (sulfide). Some gallium **compounds** emit light when an electric current passes through them.

Germanium (Ge)

Element 32 on the **periodic table**. A rare, brittle, silvery-gray **metalloid** in **group 4** (the **carbon group**). It was discovered by Clemens Winkler, a German chemist, in 1886.

Germanium is important as a **semiconductor** and is used in **silicon** chips as well as some high-quality lenses.

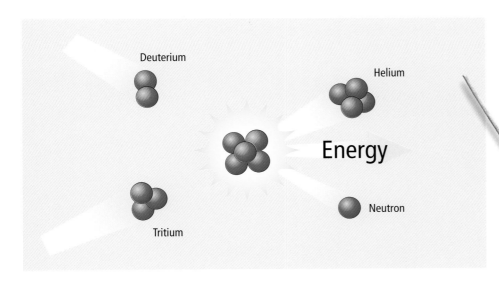

▲ **Fusion**—The deuterium-tritium fusion reaction. Deuterium and tritium are isotopes of hydrogen.

Fusion

The combining of **atoms** to form a heavier atom.

Francium (Fr)

Element 87 on the **periodic table**. The heaviest **alkali metal** (a **group 1** element).

It is a **radioactive metal** that does not occur naturally. Marguerite Perey discovered it in 1939.

G

Gadolinium (Gd)

Element 64 on the **periodic table**. A rare silvery-white and easily bent **rare-earth metal** and one of the **lanthanides**.

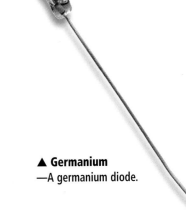

▲ **Germanium**
—A germanium diode.

Gold (Au)

Element 79 on the **periodic table**. A dense, heavy, shiny yellow **precious metal** and one of the **transition metals**.

Gold is soft and easily shaped (**malleable**)—it even makes thin sheets called gold leaf. It does not **tarnish** or **corrode**. It is found widely in pure native form, mainly in small pieces but occasionally in large nuggets. That is why it was one of the first metals ever used by people.

Its low reactivity made it most easily turned into coins.

Gold does not stand up to continual handling, so to make it useful, it is alloyed with other metals. Most gold used in jewelry is an **alloy** with **silver**, **copper**, or **zinc**. White gold is 70% silver. Gold alloys are measured in 24ths, units called carats—24-carat gold is pure gold.

Gold is a good conductor of electricity and is plated over switch contacts and other places where it is important that no corrosion occur. Gold has also long been used for tooth fillings, partly because it doesn't corrode, and partly for its decorative effect.

▲ **Gold**—Nuggets are sizable pieces of native gold, while flakes are smaller fragments. This picture shows a gold nugget and flakes.

▼ A vein carrying gold in a mine tunnel.

Group (groups 0-8)

A vertical column of **elements** on the **periodic table**. There are many ways to classify each group, and so each gets a variety of numbers and names. There is no one universal system, and what follows here is the grouping as used on the periodic table on pages 34 and 35.

▶ **Hydrogen**, a **nonmetal**, is often placed on its own and is thought of as being in group 0. On the periodic table it often appears above the **metals** in group 1.

▶ Group 1, the **alkali metals**, include **lithium** to **francium**.

▶ Group 2, the **alkaline-earth metals**, includes the elements **beryllium** to **radium**.

▶ Group 3, the **boron group**, contains **boron**, **aluminum**, **gallium**, **indium**, and **thallium**.

▶ Between groups 2 and 3 are the **transition metals** (also called **transition elements**). The transition metals include **copper** and **iron**.

▶ Group 4, the **carbon group**, contains **carbon**, **silicon**, **germanium**, **tin**, and **lead**.

▶ Group 5, the **nitrogen group**, contains **nitrogen**, **phosphorus**, **arsenic**, **antimony**, and **bismuth**.

▶ Group 6, the **oxygen group**, includes **oxygen**, **sulfur**, selenium, tellurium, and polonium.

▶ Group 7, the **halogens**, includes **fluorine**, **chlorine**, **bromine**, **iodine**, and **astatine**.

▶ Group 8, the **noble gases**, contains **helium**, **neon**, **argon**, **krypton**, **xenon**, and **radon**.

The properties of the groups change markedly from group 0 to group 8. For example:

▶ The elements of group 0 and 8 are gases that are difficult to condense.

▶ The alkali metals, in group 1, are soft, metallic solids with low melting points.

▶ The alkaline-earth metals, in group 2, are harder and have higher melting points.

▶ The hardness and melting points increase through groups 3 and 4.

▶ Hardness decreases again through groups 5, 6, and 7.

H

Hafnium (Hf)
Element 72 on the **periodic table**. A silvery, soft, bendable **metal** belonging to the **transition metals**.

It was discovered by Dirk Coster and George Charles de Hevesy in 1923, and was named after the Latin word for the city of Copenhagen (*Hafnia*).

Hafnium absorbs **neutrons** and is used for control rods in nuclear reactors. An **alloy** of **tantalum,** hafnium, and **carbon** has a very high melting point (4,215°C) and can hold other materials for melting.

Half-life
The time it takes for the **radiation** coming from a sample of a **radioactive element** to decrease by half.

Halide
A **salt** of one of the **halogens** (**fluorine**, **chlorine**, **bromine**, and **iodine**), **group 7** on the **periodic table**.

Halogen, halogen group
Fluorine (F), chlorine (Cl), bromine (Br), iodine (I), and astatine (At) are the five halogens and members of **group 7** on the **periodic table**. Fluorine is the most **reactive**.

▶ **Halogen**—The halogens are all very reactive. Here chlorine reacts with copper to produce copper chloride. This experiment was conducted in a fume chamber since chlorine is very poisonous.

▼ **Halide**—Halides readily dissolve in water. They are only precipitated when water is evaporated, such as when desert lakes dry up or in coastal lagoons. The precipitates form white crystals, most commonly seen as the white "ghost lakes" or playas in deserts, as shown here.

Hassium (Hs)
Element 108 on the **periodic table**. An artificial, **radioactive** element, also called unniloctium (Uno), belonging to the **transition metals**.

Hassium was discovered in 1984 by West German researchers at the Institute for Heavy Ion Research. It has properties similar to **osmium**, which is just above it on the periodic table. It has no practical uses. Hassium is a **transuranium element**.

Heavy elements

Elements heavier than **helium** on the **periodic table**. Elements as heavy as **iron** were formed by the **fusion** of lighter elements.

Helium (He)

Element 2 on the **periodic table**. An **inert** gas of **group 8** (the **noble gases**).

It is colorless and odorless, and the second most common and second lightest element in the universe.

Helium was discovered by the French astronomer Pierre Janssen in 1868.

Helium is too light to be common in our atmosphere, although it is found combined with natural gas. Helium is obtained by liquefying natural gas. It is the last component to liquefy.

Helium is used in balloons and as an inert gas when there would otherwise be a risk of explosion.

▼ **Helium**—Helium is used in balloons because it is lighter than air.

Holmium (Ho)

Element 67 on the **periodic table**. A **rare-earth metal** and one of the **lanthanides**.

It is highly magnetic, but it has little practical use.

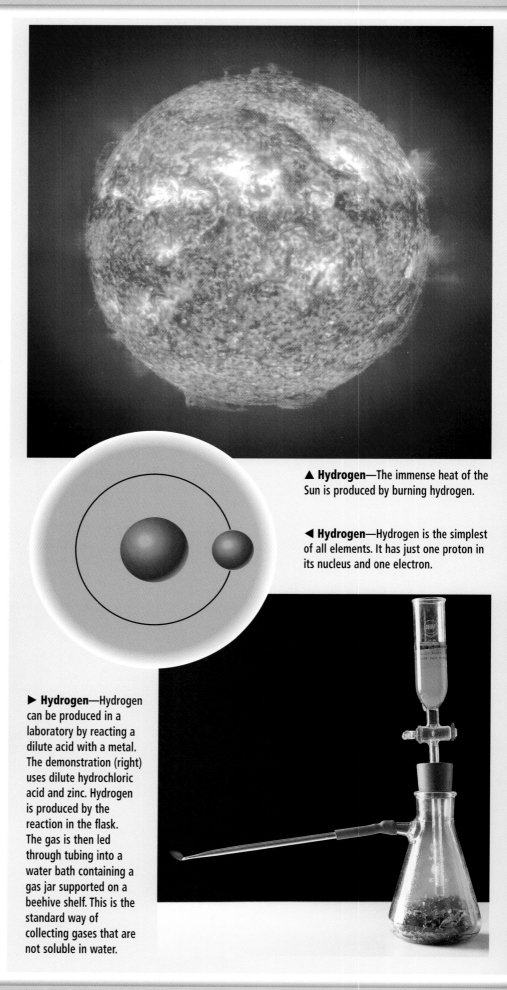

▲ **Hydrogen**—The immense heat of the Sun is produced by burning hydrogen.

◄ **Hydrogen**—Hydrogen is the simplest of all elements. It has just one proton in its nucleus and one electron.

► **Hydrogen**—Hydrogen can be produced in a laboratory by reacting a dilute acid with a metal. The demonstration (right) uses dilute hydrochloric acid and zinc. Hydrogen is produced by the reaction in the flask. The gas is then led through tubing into a water bath containing a gas jar supported on a beehive shelf. This is the standard way of collecting gases that are not soluble in water.

Hydrogen (H)

Element 1 on the **periodic table**. The most common element in the universe. It has properties like those elements in groups 1 and 8. It usually appears in **group 1** but is often placed on its own and is also thought of as being in group 0.

Hydrogen accounts for about 87% of all matter in the universe. Because it is so light, hydrogen is rare in the Earth's atmosphere. It is, however, abundant in **compounds**— for example, it makes up just over a tenth of the mass of seawater.

Hydrogen is a colorless, odorless, tasteless, flammable gas. It is the simplest of all elements, having just one **proton** in its **nucleus** and one **electron**.

Hydrogen was discovered by the English chemist Henry Cavendish in 1766. At that time it was called inflammable air or phlogiston. The name hydrogen was given by French chemist Antoine-Laurent Lavoisier from the Greek meaning "maker of water."

Hydrogen gas goes into many chemicals, including ammonia (which is then made into fertilizers). It is also used in some food, such as in margarine.

I

Indium (In)

Element 49 on the **periodic table**. A rare silvery-white **metal** belonging to **group 3** (the **boron group**).

Discovered in 1863 by Ferdinand Reich and Theodor Richter, it is very soft and can easily be made to change shape (*see:* **Malleable**). Pure indium "screams" when it is bent.

Indium is used in making electronic components.

Inert

Unreactive. The **noble gases** and **nitrogen** are examples of inert gases.

Insoluble

A substance that will not **dissolve**.

Many substances will not dissolve in one **solvent**, but will dissolve in another. Oil is insoluble in water but is **soluble** in many organic solvents.

▲ **Iodine**—The seaweed kelp is a source of natural iodine.

Iodine (I)

Element 53 on the **periodic table**. A **nonmetallic** element and one of the **halogens** (**group 7** elements).

Iodine does not occur naturally. Its **compounds** can be processed to produce pure dark-violet crystals. At room temperature solid iodine turns into a vapor (sublimes) to make an unpleasantly irritating violet vapor. It is used in medicine (a dilute **solution** of iodine in alcohol is called tincture of iodine and works as an antiseptic), in photography, and in dyes.

Iodine is one of the essential nutrients in the body. To ensure that people get enough of it, iodine is added to most table **salt**.

▼ **Iodine**—Iodine is a purple gas and solid.

Ion

An **atom**, or group of atoms, that has gained or lost one or more **electrons**, developing an electrical charge.

Ions behave differently from electrically neutral atoms and **molecules**. They can move in an electric field, and they can also bind strongly to **solvent** molecules such as water. Positively charged ions are called **cations**; negatively charged ions are called **anions**. Ions carry electrical current through **solutions**.

Ionic bond

A common type of **bond** that occurs between two **ions** when they have opposite charges (**cations** and **anions**). For example, when a salty **solution** is evaporated, **sodium** cations bond with **chloride** anions to form common table salt (sodium chloride). Ionic bonds are strong, except in the presence of a **solvent**.

(*See also:* **Covalent bond** and **Metallic bond**.)

Iridium (Ir)

Element 77 on the **periodic table**. One of the **transition metals**. It is a precious (very rare), very dense, silver-white **metal**. It is obtained as a by-product of **copper** and **nickel** refining. Iridium is so unreactive it cannot be **dissolved** by even concentrated acids unless in special combinations. It was discovered in 1803 by the English chemist Smithson Tennant. The name comes from the Greek word for rainbow because its **compounds** have a wide variety of colors.

Because it is so hard to obtain and to work, iridium is rarely used on its own. However, it does go into **platinum alloys**. The alloy is harder and resists chemical attack better than platinum alone. In its alloyed form platinum is usually used for jewelry.

▼ **Iron**—Iron and steel have been two of the most important materials for centuries. In almost any scene you will find steel. For example, steel makes the hull, railings, and chimney of the 19th-century steamboat in the foreground as well as the hull and superstructure of the tanker in the distance. The bridge deck is also supported by steel cables. The cranes are entirely made from steel. The power plant chimneys are also steel. Steel is iron with a small percentage of carbon and many of the other impurities taken out and controlled amounts of others added.

Iron (Fe)

Element 26 on the **periodic table**. A common **metal** element belonging to the **transition metals**.

Iron makes up about one-twentieth of the Earth's crust, being the second most abundant metal after **aluminum**. However, it is far easier to separate from its **compounds** than aluminum and has become the world's most useful metal. Iron is the most common magnetic element.

▲ **Iron**—This iron anchor is several hundred years old and has corroded in the warm humid coastal climate of Florida.

Iron is a steel-gray metal. It is quite **reactive** and readily **corrodes** to produce brown iron oxides, commonly known as rust.

Iron is also an important part of the human body. For example, it makes blood red.

Refined iron contains about 4% **carbon**. That makes it quite brittle. When most of the carbon is removed, it becomes easier to work. It is then called steel.

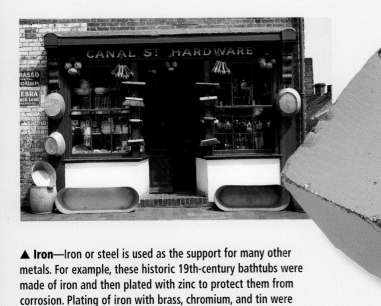

▲ **Iron**—Iron or steel is used as the support for many other metals. For example, these historic 19th-century bathtubs were made of iron and then plated with zinc to protect them from corrosion. Plating of iron with brass, chromium, and tin were common in the 19th century because plastics, aluminum, and other materials had not been commercially developed.

◀ **Iron**—Iron is found in many natural compounds, where it tends to add color. This picture shows the mineral pyrite (iron sulfide). Pyrite is also know as "fool's gold" because its color is similar to that of gold. However, it is much less dense and, unlike gold, corrodes easily in air to produce a gray powder.

Isotopes

Two or more **atoms** that have the same number of **protons** in their nucleus, but that have a different **atomic mass** because the number of **neutrons** can vary; for example, **carbon**-12 and carbon-14. **Fluorine** has only one isotope, but **elements** such as **tin** have ten. Most elements have at least two isotopes. Some isotopes are **radioactive**.

K

Krypton (Kr)

Element 36 on the **periodic table**. One of the **noble gases** from **group 8**.

It is an **inert** gas and forms very few **compounds**.

Krypton is heavier than air, colorless, odorless, and tasteless. Krypton was discovered in 1898 by the British chemists Sir William Ramsay and Morris W. Travers.

Krypton is used in some types of fluorescent lamps. When a current of electricity is passed through a glass tube containing krypton at low pressure, it gives out a bluish-white light.

L

Lanthanum (La)

Element 57 on the **periodic table**. A member of the **rare-earth metals** and one of the **lanthanides**.

Lanthanum is a soft, silvery-white **metal** that is easy to bend (**malleable**). It was discovered in 1839 by Carl Gustaf Mosander. Its name comes from a Greek word meaning "to be concealed" because it was particularly difficult to separate from its **compounds**. Lanthanum oxide is used in high-quality glass lenses.

Lanthanide

An **element** belonging to the lanthanide **series**—17 similar metallic elements starting with **scandium** (21) and **yttrium** (39) and including the elements from **lanthanum** (57) to **lutetium** (71) in **period 6** on the **periodic table**. The lanthanides are also called **rare-earth metals** or **rare-earth elements**, and they are **transition metals**.

Lavoisier, Antoine-Laurent

A French chemist who, in 1789, published the first list of **elements**, following the definition of an element by Robert **Boyle**.

Lavoisier's list contains some substances (lime, alumina, and silica) that we now know as **compounds** because he did not have ways to separate them. He also included light and heat (known as caloric) on his list.

(*See also:* **Hydrogen**; **Nitrogen**; **Oxygen**.)

Lawrencium (Lr)

Element 103 on the **periodic table**. An artificial and **radioactive** element of the **actinide series**.

It was produced in 1961 by Albert Ghiorso, T. Sikkeland, A. E. Larsh, and R. M. Latimer. Lawrencium is a **transuranium element**.

Lead (Pb)

Element 82 on the **periodic table**. A soft, silvery-white **metal** in **group 4** (the **carbon group**).

Lead is very dense, soft, and easily shaped (**malleable**). It is also a poor conductor of electricity. When lead is exposed to air, it quickly develops a coating that turns it dull brown.

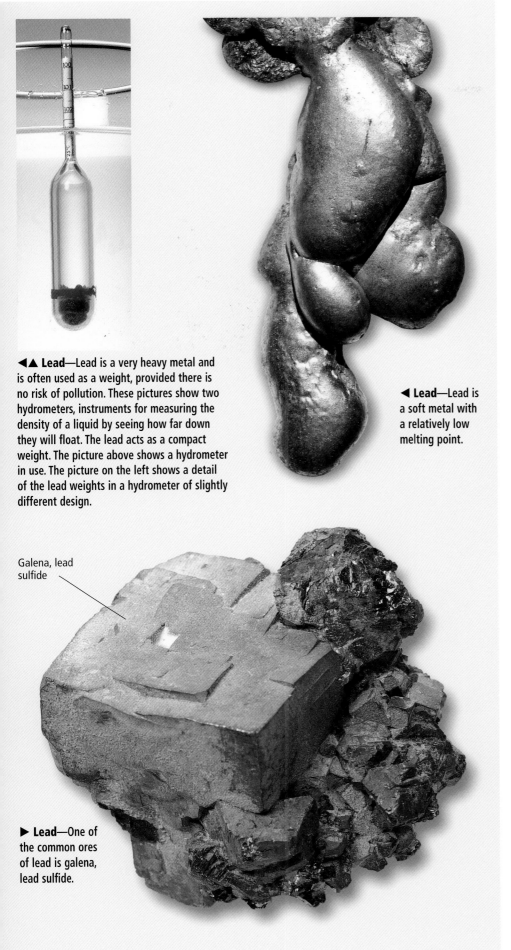

◀▲ **Lead**—Lead is a very heavy metal and is often used as a weight, provided there is no risk of pollution. These pictures show two hydrometers, instruments for measuring the density of a liquid by seeing how far down they will float. The lead acts as a compact weight. The picture above shows a hydrometer in use. The picture on the left shows a detail of the lead weights in a hydrometer of slightly different design.

◀ **Lead**—Lead is a soft metal with a relatively low melting point.

Galena, lead sulfide

▶ **Lead**—One of the common ores of lead is galena, lead sulfide.

This coating (similar in effect to the coating that develops on copper) then helps prevent further **reaction**, and so **corrosion** happens very slowly. This has made it suitable as a roofing material and to protect underground cables. In the past it was made into water pipes. Lead also goes into making the plates for storage batteries, such as those in cars.

It makes low-melting point **alloys**, such as solder, and pewter. Lead will absorb and protect from sound and **radiation**. At one time it went into an antiknock ingredient in gasoline. But it is poisonous and so now has been taken out of gas and water pipes.

Lead is mainly found in the **mineral** lead sulfide (also called galena).

Light elements

Hydrogen and **helium** on the **periodic table**.

Lithium (Li)

Element 3 on the **periodic table**. A member of the **alkali metals** (**group 1** elements).

Lithium is a soft, white, shiny **metal**. It was discovered in 1817 by Johan August Arfwedson.

Lithium is **alloyed** with **aluminum**, **lead**, and other soft metals to make them harder. It is also used in some batteries.

Lutetium (Lu)

Element 71 on the **periodic table**. A **transition metal** belonging to the **lanthanides** and also a **rare-earth metal**.

Lutetium was discovered in 1907 by Carl Auer von Welsbach and Georges Urbain. The name for the element comes from the Latin word for Paris. It has no important practical use.

M

Magnesium (Mg)

Element 12 on the **periodic table**. A silvery-white, soft, and **reactive** member of the **alkaline-earth metals (group 2** elements).

It is the eighth most common element in the Earth's crust. Magnesium is also important in the human body. It is the lightest metal that is common in construction and is widely used in aircraft and space vehicles. It is **alloyed** with **aluminum**, **zinc**, and **manganese** to improve their strength.

Compounds of magnesium are medicines, such as epsom salts (magnesium sulfate) and milk of magnesia (magnesium carbonate).

Magnesium was discovered in 1808 by English scientist Sir Humphry Davy.

▲ **Magnesium**—The mineral dolomite is a carbonate of magnesium and calcium.

Malleable

Able to be beaten or rolled into a new shape. Applies to **metals**. (*See also:* **Ductile**.)

▲ **Magnesium**—Magnesium is the most reactive of the metals that can be used in everyday applications. When a taper of magnesium ribbon is lit, it rapidly bursts into flame, giving out a bright white light. This is used in signal flares.

Manganese (Mn)

Element 25 on the **periodic table**. A silvery-white, hard, brittle **metal** belonging to the **transition metals**.

Discovered in 1774 by the Swedish chemist Carl Wilhelm Scheele, manganese mainly is used to make steel easier to work. Manganese steel is also hard wearing and **corrosion** resistant.

Mass

The amount of **matter** in an object. In everyday use the word weight is often used to mean mass.

Matter

Anything that takes up space.

Meitnerium (Mt)

Element 109 on the **periodic table**. An artificially produced **radioactive** element, also called unnilennium (Une), belonging to the **transition metals**. It is a **transuranium element** discovered in 1982 at the Institute for Heavy Ion Research in Germany when **bismuth**-209 was bombarded with **iron**-58 **ions**. Only a single nucleus of the element has so far been produced.

Mendelevium (Md)
Element 101 on the **periodic table**. An artificial and **radioactive** element in the **actinide series**. It was discovered by Albert Ghiorso, Bernard G. Harvey, Gregory R. Choppin, Stanley G. Thompson, and Glenn T. Seaborg, and named after Dmitri Ivanovitch **Mendeleev**. It is a **transuranium element**.

Mendeleev, Dmitri I.
A Russian chemist, Dmitri Ivanovitch Mendeleev (1834-1907) created the **periodic table** of the **elements**. He was convinced that the key to ordering the elements lay in their atomic weights (*see: Atomic mass*).

At the time, there were only 57 known elements. When he arranged them in the sequence of increasing atomic weights, he noted that the chemical properties of the elements were grouped into already familiar families.

To make his table work, he discovered that he had to leave spaces in it. But the spaces in the table predicted the properties of the as yet unknown elements that should be in them. As new elements were discovered, their properties were found to fit exactly into the empty spaces. The periodic table of the elements also

showed scientists where to look to discover new elements.

Mercury (Hg)
Element 80 on the **periodic table**. A silvery liquid **metal**, also called quicksilver, belonging to the **transition metals**. It has been known since ancient times.

It is occasionally found as a native liquid metal, but much more commonly as the red **mineral** cinnabar.

Mercury is the only metal element that is liquid at room temperature. In this form it is used in thermometers. It has very good electrical conductivity and goes into sealed switches. When electricity passes through mercury vapor, it gives off a bluish glow. The vapor is used in street lighting and in fluorescent lamps. Mercury is also **alloyed** with many metals.

Mercury vapor is poisonous. It once was used in hat making, and its effect on hatters gave rise to the term "mad as a hatter."

(*See also:* **Amalgam**.)

Metal, metallic element
An **element** that is a good conductor of electricity and heat, has a metallic luster, is **malleable** and **ductile**, forms **cations**, and has **oxides** that are bases.

Metals are formed as cations held together by a "sea" of **electrons**. A metal may also be an **alloy** of these elements. Examples of metals are **sodium**, **calcium**, and **gold**.

Metallic bond
A type of chemical **bond** found in solid **metals**. A metal is made of closely packed **cations** embedded in a "sea" of **electrons** that bond the **ions** together.

Every ion is surrounded by six others to make a hexagonal pattern of packing, and this gives metals their high densities. The strong bonds between the ions and the free electrons allow metals to be good conductors of heat and electricity, and means that they are not brittle.

(*See also:* **Covalent bond** and **Ionic bond**.)

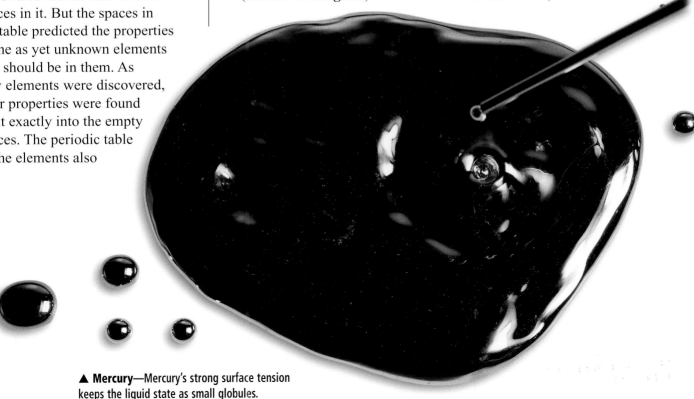

▲ **Mercury**—Mercury's strong surface tension keeps the liquid state as small globules.

Metalloid

A class of **elements** intermediate in properties between **metals** and **nonmetals**.

Metalloids are also called semimetals or **semiconductors**. Examples of metalloids are **silicon**, **germanium**, and **antimony**.

Mineral

A solid substance made of just one **element** or chemical **compound**.

Calcite is a mineral because it consists only of **calcium** carbonate; halite is a mineral because it contains only **sodium** chloride; quartz is a mineral because it consists only of **silicon** dioxide.

Molecule

A group of two or more **atoms** held together by chemical **bonds**.

Molybdenum (Mo)

Element 42 on the **periodic table**. A rare, silver-gray **metal** belonging to the **transition metals**.

It was named from the Greek word for "lead" because it looks like **lead**. It is used as an **alloy** to strengthen and increase the melting point of steel. It also improves **corrosion** resistance.

N

Neodymium (Nd)

Element 60 on the **periodic table**. A silvery-white **rare-earth metal** and one of the **lanthanides**.

It is used to color glass. Neodymium glass can replace a ruby inside a laser.

Neon (Ne)

Element 10 on the **periodic table**. A colorless, odorless, and tasteless **inert** gas of **group 8** (the **noble gases**).

Neon was discovered (1898) by the British chemists Sir William

▲ **Neon**—All lights in discharge tubes are generally called "neon"; however, neon only emits a reddish-orange glow. Each of the noble gases produces a different "neon" color. For example, helium produces a yellow "neon" light when an electric current flows through it.

Ramsay and Morris W. Travers. Neon forms no stable **compounds**. Its main use is in "neon" signs and fluorescent bulbs.

Neptunium (Np)

Element 93 on the **periodic table**. A silver-colored **radioactive** element of the **actinide series**.

In 1940 it became the first **transuranium element** to be artificially produced.

Neutron

A particle inside the nucleus of an **atom** that is neutral (has no charge).

▲ **Nitrogen**—Nitrogen is inert in the air; but when it forms compounds in the soil, it is an invaluable source of nourishment for plants—as shown in the fertilizer stick.

▶ **Nitrogen**—Nitrogen is an unreactive substance unless a large amount of energy is used. This shows the combustion of ammonium dichromate, a nitrogen-containing compound.

Nickel (Ni)

Element 28 on the **periodic table**. A silvery, hard, magnetic **transition metal** element.

Nickel is similar to **iron** in many of its properties, but it reacts more slowly and resists **corrosion**. It was discovered in 1751 by a Swedish chemist, Baron Axel Fredrik Cronstedt.

It is one of the main metals in "silver" coins. However, the jeweler's "nickel silver" contains no silver at all. Nickel is widely used in **alloys**.

An alloy of nickel and iron produces stainless steel. It is also used as a protective coating on steel.

Niobium (Nb)

Element 41 on the **periodic table**. A soft, easily shaped (**malleable**) **metal** belonging to the **transition metals**.

Niobium looks like steel, but seems more like **platinum** when polished. It is used in **alloys**, in particular in some stainless steels to provide extra strength. It was first discovered in 1801 by the English chemist Charles Hatchett.

Nitrogen (N)

Element 7 on the **periodic table**. An inert, colorless, odorless, and tasteless gas, and **nonmetallic** element of **group 5** (the **nitrogen group**).

It is the most common element in the atmosphere and found in all living matter.

Nitrogen was discovered by Daniel Rutherford in 1772. The French chemist Antoine **Lavoisier** named it *azote* because no living thing could survive in it (from the Greek word meaning "no life"). This term is still used in French. The name "nitrogen" was coined in 1790 after a common **mineral** then know as nitre (potassium nitrate) from "nitre" and "-gen," meaning "nitre-forming."

Nitrogen is the sixth most common element in the universe. It makes up over three-quarters of the Earth's atmosphere.

Nitrogen is removed (fixed) from the atmosphere by bacteria living on the roots of some plants such as peas, usually called legumes. Animals then get nitrogen for their tissues by eating vegetable or animal proteins.

Nitrogen is made by liquefying air. It is widely used to keep air away from food during food preparation. Freeze-drying is done in an atmosphere of nitrogen.

Oxides of nitrogen are poisonous. Nitrogen dioxide is one of the main pollutants of the atmosphere and a producer of ground-level ozone.

Nitrogen group elements

The **group 5 elements** on the **periodic table**, which include **nitrogen (N)**, **phosphorus (P)**, **arsenic (As)**, **antimony (Sb)**, and **bismuth (Bi)**.

Nitrogen and phosphorus are two of the vital constituents in all living things.

Nobelium (No)

Element 102 on the **periodic table**. An artificial and **radioactive** element of the **actinide series**.

It was discovered in 1958 by Albert Ghiorso, T. Sikkeland, J.R. Walton, and Glenn T. Seaborg. It is a **transuranium element**.

Noble gases

The members of **group 8** on the **periodic table** (from top to bottom) **helium (He)**, **neon (Ne)**, **argon (Ar)**, **krypton (Kr)**, **xenon (Xe)**, and **radon (Rn)**.

These gases are almost entirely **inert**.

Noble metals

Gold (Au), **iridium (Ir)**, **osmium (Os)**, **palladium (Pd)**, **platinum (Pt)**, **rhenium (Rh)**, **rhodium (Rh)**, **ruthenium (Ru)**, and **silver (Ag)**.

They are the least **reactive metals**. (*See also:* **Reactivity series**.)

Nonferrous

Metals other than **iron** and steel, for example, **aluminum**.

Nonmetals

Brittle substances that do not conduct electricity. Examples include **sulfur**, **phosphorus**, and all the gases.

Nuclear reactions

Reactions that occur in the core, or nucleus, of an **atom**.

O

Osmium (Os)

Element 76 on the **periodic table**. A gray-white **metal**, the densest naturally occurring element. Osmium belongs to the **transition metals**.

Osmium is hard and brittle. It was once made into filaments in electric light bulbs, but has now been replaced by **tungsten**. The English chemist Smithson Tennant discovered it in 1804. Osmium is known for the unpleasant (and poisonous) odor of some of its **compounds**.

Oxide

A **compound** that includes **oxygen** and one other **element**. (*See also:* **Corrosion, corrode**.)

Oxidize

To combine with or gain more **oxygen**.

▼ **Oxygen**—Oxygen is an important gas for combustion. Here a stick of carbon is strongly ignited when a flow of pure oxygen is applied through a test tube. With just the oxygen in the air the carbon would simply glow.

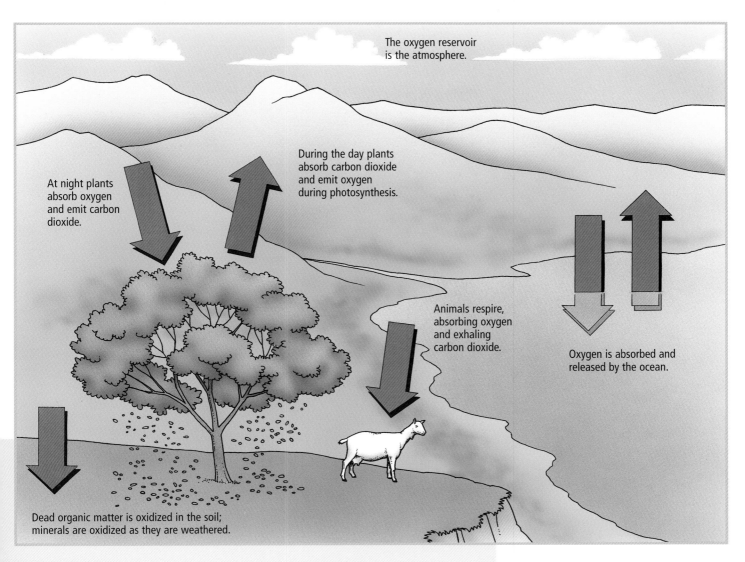

The oxygen reservoir is the atmosphere.

At night plants absorb oxygen and emit carbon dioxide.

During the day plants absorb carbon dioxide and emit oxygen during photosynthesis.

Animals respire, absorbing oxygen and exhaling carbon dioxide.

Oxygen is absorbed and released by the ocean.

Dead organic matter is oxidized in the soil; minerals are oxidized as they are weathered.

Oxygen (O)

Element 8 on the **periodic table**. A **nonmetallic** chemical element of **group 6** (the **oxygen group**).

Oxygen is the most common gas in the atmosphere after **nitrogen**, making up just over one-fifth of the Earth's atmosphere. It is the third most abundant element in the universe after **hydrogen** and **helium**. It is a colorless, tasteless, and odorless gas. Oxygen reacts with many elements to produce **oxides**. The most common oxide is water.

Oxygen was discovered in 1772 by the Swedish chemist Carl Wilhelm Scheele and independently by the English chemist Joseph Priestley in 1774.

▲ Oxygen—The oxygen cycle.

The French chemist Antoine Lavoisier gave oxygen its name.

Oxygen makes up 89% by weight of seawater and 47% by weight of the Earth's crust. It is vital for almost all forms of life. Animals take in oxygen and give out carbon dioxide. Plants take in carbon dioxide and give out oxygen. As a result, almost all of the oxygen in the atmosphere is from plants (the process is called photosynthesis). Some uncombined oxygen **dissolves** in water, providing the oxygen needed for marine animals.

Oxygen is manufactured by liquefying air.

Oxygen group elements

The **group 6 elements** on the **periodic table** (also includes the **chalcogens**). The members of the group are (from top to bottom) **oxygen (O)**, **sulfur (S)**, **selenium (Se)**, **tellurium (Te)**, and **polonium (Po)**.

P

Palladium (Pd)

Element 46 on the **periodic table**. This gray-white **metal** is a light **transition metal**.

It is used to increase the speed of chemical **reactions** (it is a **catalyst**). It does not **corrode**, and it mainly appears in electrical contacts in telephone equipment.

Period

One of 7 rows of **elements** on the **periodic table**.

The most **metallic** elements are to the left, and the most **nonmetallic** elements are to the right.

Periodic table (of the elements)

A chart that organizes **elements** by **atomic number** and chemical properties into **groups** and **periods**. It was started by Dmitri Ivanovich **Mendeleev**.

▼ **Periodic table (of the elements)**—The periodic table is a system of classification that allows the elements to be arranged, in order of atomic number, into groups of elements with similar properties. The table contains a great deal of information on each element.

GROUPS ▶

PERIODS ▼

	1 (1)	2 (2)	Transition metals					(8)
			(3)	(4)	(5)	(6)	(7)	
1	1 **H** Hydrogen 1							
2	3 **Li** Lithium 7	4 **Be** Beryllium 9						
3	11 **Na** Sodium 23	12 **Mg** Magnesium 24						
4	19 **K** Potassium 39	20 **Ca** Calcium 40	21 **Sc** Scandium 45	22 **Ti** Titanium 48	23 **V** Vanadium 51	24 **Cr** Chromium 52	25 **Mn** Manganese 55	26 **Fe** Iron 56
5	37 **Rb** Rubidium 85	38 **Sr** Strontium 88	39 **Y** Yttrium 89	40 **Zr** Zirconium 91	41 **Nb** Niobium 93	42 **Mo** Molybdenum 96	43 **Tc** Technetium (99)	44 **Ru** Ruthen 10
6	55 **Cs** Cesium 133	56 **Ba** Barium 137	71 **Lu** Lutetium 175	72 **Hf** Hafnium 178	73 **Ta** Tantalum 181	74 **W** Tungsten 184	75 **Re** Rhenium 186	76 **O** Osmiu 190
7	87 **Fr** Francium (223)	88 **Ra** Radium (226)	103 **Lr** Lawrencium (260)	104 **Rf** Rutherfordium (261)	105 **Db** Dubnium (262)	106 **Sg** Seaborgium (263)	107 **Bh** Bohrium (262)	108 **H** Hassiu (26

Lanthanide series

57 **La** Lanthanum 139	58 **Ce** Cerium 140	59 **Pr** Praseodymium 141	60 **N** Neodym 14

Actinide series

89 **Ac** Actinium (227)	90 **Th** Thorium (232)	91 **Pa** Protactinium (231)	92 **U** Uraniu (238

■ **Metals**

□ **Metalloids (semimetals)**

■ **Nonmetals**

■ **Inner transition metals**

Atomic (proton) number (equivalent to number of electrons).
For a definition see page 6.

13
Al
Aluminum
27

— Symbol

— Name

Approximate relative atomic mass (approximate atomic weight).
For a definition see page 39. Those in parentheses are radioactive.

				3	**4**	**5**	**6**	**7**	**8 or 0**
(9)	(10)	(11)	(12)	(13)	(14)	(15)	(16)	(17)	(18)
									2 **He** Helium 4
				5 **B** Boron 11	6 **C** Carbon 12	7 **N** Nitrogen 14	8 **O** Oxygen 16	9 **F** Fluorine 19	10 **Ne** Neon 20
				13 **Al** Aluminum 27	14 **Si** Silicon 28	15 **P** Phosphorus 31	16 **S** Sulfur 32	17 **Cl** Chlorine 35	18 **Ar** Argon 40
27 **Co** Cobalt 59	28 **Ni** Nickel 59	29 **Cu** Copper 64	30 **Zn** Zinc 65	31 **Ga** Gallium 70	32 **Ge** Germanium 73	33 **As** Arsenic 75	34 **Se** Selenium 79	35 **Br** Bromine 80	36 **Kr** Krypton 84
45 **Rh** Rhodium 103	46 **Pd** Palladium 106	47 **Ag** Silver 108	48 **Cd** Cadmium 112	49 **In** Indium 115	50 **Sn** Tin 119	51 **Sb** Antimony 122	52 **Te** Tellurium 128	53 **I** Iodine 127	54 **Xe** Xenon 131
77 **Ir** Iridium 192	78 **Pt** Platinum 195	79 **Au** Gold 197	80 **Hg** Mercury 201	81 **Tl** Thallium 204	82 **Pb** Lead 207	83 **Bi** Bismuth 209	84 **Po** Polonium (209)	85 **At** Astatine (210)	86 **Rn** Radon (222)
109 **Mt** Meitnerium (266)	110 **Uun** Ununnilium (272)	111 **Uuu** Unununium (272)	112 **Uub** Ununbium (277)		114 **Uuq** Ununquadium (289)		116 **Uuh** Ununhexium (289)		118 **Uuo** Ununoctium (293)

| 61 **Pm** Promethium (145) | 62 **Sm** Samarium 150 | 63 **Eu** Europium 152 | 64 **Gd** Gadolinium 157 | 65 **Tb** Terbium 159 | 66 **Dy** Dysprosium 163 | 67 **Ho** Holmium 165 | 68 **Er** Erbium 167 | 69 **Tm** Thulium 169 | 70 **Yb** Ytterbium 173 |
| 93 **Np** Neptunium (237) | 94 **Pu** Plutonium (244) | 95 **Am** Americium (243) | 96 **Cm** Curium (247) | 97 **Bk** Berkelium (247) | 98 **Cf** Californium (251) | 99 **Es** Einsteinium (252) | 100 **Fm** Fermium (257) | 101 **Md** Mendelevium (258) | 102 **No** Nobelium (259) |

Phosphorus (P)

Element 15 on the **periodic table**. A member of **group 5** (the **nitrogen group**).

There are three forms of phosphorus: white, red, and black. Most commonly it is a colorless, soft, waxy solid that glows in the dark. It is highly **reactive** in air and catches fire spontaneously. It was discovered by Hennig Brand in 1669 from the remains of evaporated urine. Phosphorus is present in all living cells.

White phosphorus has been used to make incendiary (burning) bombs. Red phosphorus is used for the striking surface of safety matches.

Platinum (Pt)

Element 78 on the **periodic table**. A soft, easily worked (**malleable**), and very heavy, silver-white **metal**. It is one of the **transition metals**.

It was discovered by Julius Caesar Scaliger in 1557. The Spaniards found it in the river deposits of the Río Pinto,

▲ **Phosphorus**—Matches show the ignition power of phosphorus compounds.

Colombia, and they named it *platina del Pinto* because it looked like silver.

Platinum has a high melting point and **corrodes** only very slowly. It is regarded as a **precious metal** and is used in jewelry and in dentistry. It is also an agent that speeds up chemical **reactions** (a **catalyst**) in the catalytic converters in car exhausts.

(*See also:* **Rhodium**.)

Plutonium (Pu)

Element 94 on the **periodic table**. A **radioactive** element of the **actinide series**.

It is the most important **transuranium element** because it can be a fuel in nuclear reactors or part of nuclear weapons. It was discovered in 1940 by Glenn T. Seaborg, Joseph W. Kennedy, and Arthur C. Wahl.

Plutonium is particularly

▼ **Potassium**—Potassium is found in ashes as the compound potash, or potassium carbonate. It is one of the most important soil nutrients.

dangerous because it emits **radiation** that is absorbed by bone marrow, one of the results of which can be leukemia.

(*See also:* **Americium**.)

Polonium (Po)

Element 84 on the **periodic table**. A **radioactive**, silvery-gray **metal** of **group 6** (the **oxygen group**).

It was the first radioactive element to be discovered, in 1898 by Pierre and Marie Curie. Polonium is very rare.

Praseodymium (Pr)

Element 59 on the **periodic table**. This silvery-colored, soft **metal** is one of the **rare-earth metals** and a **lanthanide**.

Discovered in 1885 by Carl Auer von Welsbach, it is used as an **alloy** in high-strength metals.

Precious metal

The **elements gold (Au)**, **iridium (Ir)**, **osmium (Os)**, **palladium (Pd)**, **platinum (Pt)**, **rhodium (Rh)**, **ruthenium (Ru)**, and **silver (Ag)**. All of these **metals** have similar properties and occur in adjacent positions on the **periodic table** as well as being found together in nature.

The precious metals are very rare and are found in amounts equal to less than one part per million in the Earth's crust. However, many metals are very rare. A precious metal is not only rare, but also belongs to the group of **noble metals**—the most unreactive of all the metals.

Potassium (K)

Element 19 on the **periodic table**. A soft, white, **reactive metal** and an element of **group 1** (the **alkali metals**).

It is found in all living matter. The pure metal, however, has little direct use.

Potassium was discovered in 1807 by the English chemist Sir Humphry Davy.

▲ **Potassium**—Potassium is a reactive metal. Here it burns on the surface of water.

▶ **Potassium**—Potassium is a vital element in giving some minerals their character. Muscovite, for example, is potassium aluminum silicate. It differs from many other minerals based on aluminum and silicon by the presence of the potassium.

Promethium (Pm)

Element 61 on the **periodic table**. This **radioactive metal** is one of the **rare-earth metals** and a **lanthanide**. It was discovered in 1947 by J. A. Marinsky, L. E. Glendenin, and C. D. Coryell.

Protactinium (Pa)

Element 91 on the **periodic table**. A **radioactive** chemical element of the **actinide series**.

It was discovered in 1913 by Kasimir Fajans and O.H. Göhring.

Proton

A positively charged particle in the nucleus of an **atom** that balances out the charge of the surrounding **electrons**.

R

Radiation

The exchange of energy with the surroundings by means of particles of energy.

▼ **Radiation**—This diagram shows the main sources of background radiation that most of us experience.

Radioactive

Emitting **radiation** or particles from the nucleus of **atoms**. (*See also:* **Radioactive decay**.)

Radioactive decay

A change in a **radioactive element** due to loss of **mass** through **radiation**. For example, **uranium** decays (or changes) to **lead**. (*See also:* **Half-life**.)

Radioisotope

A shortened version of the phrase **radioactive isotope**.

Radium (Ra)

Element 88 on the **periodic table**. This silvery-white **metal** is the heaviest **radioactive** element in **group 2** (the **alkaline-earth metals**).

Radium was discovered in 1889 by Pierre Curie, Marie Curie, and G. Bémon.

Radium found an important use in medicine as a way of treating cancer by focusing **radiation** on tumors. In recent times it has been replaced by **cobalt**-60.

Radium glows in the dark and was mixed with zinc sulfide to make luminous paint. This stopped when the dangers of using radium were recognized.

Radon (Rn)

Element 86 on the **periodic table**. A heavy **radioactive** gas of **group 8** (the **noble gases**).

It is produced by the **radioactive decay** of **radium**.

Radon is a colorless, odorless, tasteless gas. The atmosphere contains small amounts of radon, especially above rocks like granite as a result of seepage from the radioactive decay of **uranium** in these rocks. High levels of radon gas may be a health hazard.

Rare-earth metal, rare-earth element

An **element** belonging to a **series** of 17 chemically similar **metals** also known as **lanthanides** on the **periodic table**.

They are **cerium (Ce)**, **dysprosium (Dy)**, **erbium (Er)**, **europium (Eu)**, **gadolinium (Gd)**, **holmium (Ho)**, **lutetium(Lu)**, **lanthanum (La)**, **neodymium (Nd)**, **praseodymium (Pr)**, **promethium (Pm)**, **samarium (Sm)**, **scandium (Sc)**, **terbium (Tb)**, **thulium (Tm)**, **ytterbium (Yb)**, and **yttrium (Y)**.

Reaction

The combination of two substances using parts of each to produce new substances. For example, the reactants sodium chloride and sulfuric acid react and combine to produce sodium sulfate, chlorine, and water. (*See also:* **Catalyst**.)

Reactivity, reactive

The tendency for a substance to react with other substances. The term is most widely used in comparing the reactivity of **metals**.

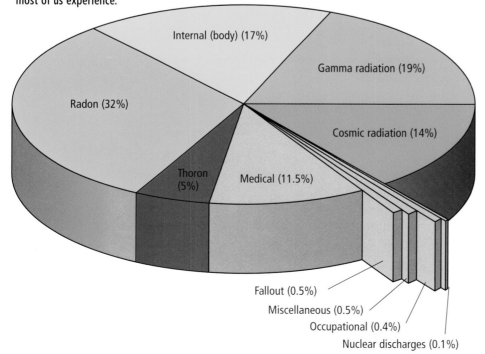

Internal (body) (17%)
Gamma radiation (19%)
Radon (32%)
Cosmic radiation (14%)
Thoron (5%)
Medical (11.5%)
Fallout (0.5%)
Miscellaneous (0.5%)
Occupational (0.4%)
Nuclear discharges (0.1%)

Metals are arranged in the **reactivity series**.

(*See also:* **Fluorine**.)

Reactivity series

The series of **metals** organized in order of their **reactivity**, with the most reactive metals, such as **potassium**, at the top and the least reactive metals, such as **platinum**, at the bottom. **Hydrogen** is usually included in the series for comparative purposes.

Reduce, reduction

To remove **oxygen** from or add **hydrogen** to a **compound**.

Relative atomic mass

In the past, a measure of the **mass** of an **atom** on a scale relative to the mass of an atom of **hydrogen**, where hydrogen has an **atomic mass** of 1.

Nowadays, a measure of the mass of an atom is made relative to the mass of one-twelfth of an atom of **carbon**-12. If the relative atomic mass is given as a rounded figure, it is called an approximate relative atomic mass. For example, the approximate relative atomic mass of chlorine is 35, calcium 40, and gold 197.

Rhenium (Re)

Element 75 on the **periodic table**. A very dense element and one of the **transition metals**.

It was discovered in 1925 by the German chemists Ida and Walter Noddack and Otto Carl Berg. It has few direct uses.

Rhodium (Rh)

Element 45 on the **periodic table**. A rare, silver-white member of the **transition metals**.

Rhodium is normally obtained as a by-product from the refining of **copper** and **nickel**. It is a **precious**

Reactivity series	
Elements	**Reactivity**
Potassium	Most reactive
Sodium	
Calcium	
Magnesium	
Aluminum	
Manganese	
Chromium	
Zinc	
Iron	
Cadmium	
Tin	
Lead	
Hydrogen	
Copper	
Mercury	
Silver	
Gold	
Platinum	Least reactive

◄ **Reactivity series**—Because metals differ in their reactivity, if a more reactive metal is placed in a solution of a less reactive metal compound, a reaction occurs that takes the reactive metal into solution and forces the less reactive metal out of solution, forming a precipitate. This important reaction is used in refining some metals.

▼ **Reactivity series**—Copper is more reactive than silver. A copper strip placed in a silver nitrate solution causes the silver to be precipitated onto the copper strip.

metal and will not **tarnish**. It is often electroplated as a coating onto other metals to make a shiny, nontarnishing finish on tableware and jewelry. Its other main use is as an **alloying** metal to make **platinum** harder.

Rubidium (Rb)

Element 37 on the **periodic table**. A member of **group 1** (the **alkali metals**). This silvery **metal** is the second most **reactive** metal. Rubidium reacts spontaneously in air and water. When it reacts with water, it releases **hydrogen gas**, which then catches fire.

It was discovered in 1861 by Robert Bunsen and Gustav Kirchhoff. It is named after the red color that can been seen in a spectrometer. It has to be kept in dry mineral oil or in a hydrogen atmosphere.

Ruthenium (Ru)

Element 44 on the **periodic table**. A silver-gray colored **metal** and member of the **transition metals**. It is used to make **alloys** harder. It was discovered in 1844 by the Russian chemist Karl Karlovich Klaus.

Rutherfordium (Rf)

Element 104 on the **periodic table**. An artificial **radioactive** element, also called unnilquadium (Unq), belonging to the **transition metals**. It was discovered in 1964 at the Joint Institute for Nuclear Research at Dubna, Russia. It has no practical uses. Rutherfordium is a **transuranium element**.

S

Salt

A **compound**, often involving a **metal**, that is the result of a **reaction** between an acid and a base or between two **elements**. "Salt" is also the common word for **sodium** chloride—common salt or table salt.

Samarium (Sm)

Element 62 on the **periodic table**. A silvery-white **metal** belonging to the **rare-earth metals** and one of the **lanthanides**. Samarium was discovered in 1879 by Paul-Émile Lecoq de Boisbaudran. It has few uses.

Scandium (Sc)

Element 21 on the **periodic table**. A soft, silvery-white **metal**, the first member of the **rare-earth metals**, and one of the **lanthanides**. It was discovered in 1879 by Lars Fredrik Nilson. It has an unusually low density and high melting point, but few uses have so far been found for it.

Seaborgium (Sg)

Element 106 on the **periodic table**. An artificial **radioactive** element, also called unnilhexium (Unh), belonging to the **transition metals**.

It has properties similar to **tungsten**, which is just above it on the periodic table. It was discovered in 1974 by Georgy N. Flerov. It has no practical uses. Seaborgium is a **transuranium element**.

Selenium (Se)

Element 34 on the **periodic table**. A **metalloid** in **group 6** (the **oxygen group**).

It was discovered in 1818 by the Swedish chemist Jöns Jacob Berzelius.

It has the unusual property that it conducts electricity much better when light falls on it. It can also convert light into electricity. For these reasons it is used in photoelectric and solar cells. It also goes into red enamels and strengthens rubber.

Semiconductor

A material of low electrical conductivity. Conductivity increases with temperature.

Semiconductor devices often use **silicon** when they are made as part of diodes, transistors, or integrated circuits.

Elements lying between **metals** and **nonmetals** are also sometimes called semiconductors. Examples of semiconductors are silicon, germanium **oxide**, and **germanium**.

(*See also:* **Doping** and **Metalloid**.)

Semimetal

(*See:* **Metalloid**.)

Series

A sequence of **elements** that have similar or related characteristics.

It may also be a part of a **period** (row) on the **periodic table** such as the **actinide** or **lanthanide** series.

▼ **Selenium**—This is a bank of photocells that use selenium as a light-sensitive electrical generator.

Shell, shell diagrams

The term or diagram used to describe the imaginary surfaces outside the nucleus of an **atom** that would be formed by a set of **electrons** of similar energy. The outermost shell is known as the valence shell. For example, **neon** has shells containing two and eight electrons.

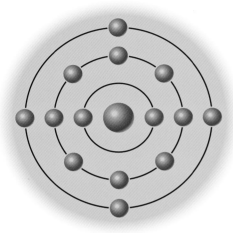

▲ **Shell, shell diagrams**—This is a shell diagram for the element silicon. It contains 2 electrons in its inner shell, 8 in the middle shell, and 4 in the outer shell. The nucleus is in the center. This is only a convenient representation—real elements do not look like this.

▶ **Silicon**—Glass is an amorphous form of silica, meaning that it has not formed any true crystals. That is why it is transparent.

▼ **Silicon**—Most silicon is found in the form of silicates—compounds of silicon and oxygen. This is the mineral agate, a silicate colored orange by atoms of iron.

Silicon (Si)

Element 14 on the **periodic table**. A **metalloid** in **group 4** (the **carbon group**). Silicon forms about 28% of the Earth's crust, making it the second most common element in the crust after **oxygen**.

Silicon was discovered in 1824 by the Swedish chemist Jöns Jacob Berzelius. It does not occur uncombined, but always with oxygen as silicates and other **minerals**. Quartz is a **compound** of silicon and oxygen. Sand and clay are also compounds dominated by silica.

Pure silicon is a hard, dark gray solid. It is unreactive with water or acids and so is used widely to make containers. It is the main component in glass.

The atomic structure of silicon has made it a very important **semiconductor**. It is the basis of "silicon chips." (*See also:* **Arsenic**.)

Silver (Ag)

Element 47 on the **periodic table**. A soft, silvery **metal** belonging to the **transition metals**.

Silver is one of the **precious metals**. It is common in jewelry (but not in modern "silver" coins). Silver is also an excellent conductor of electricity. It is **alloyed** with elements such as **nickel** to make electrical contacts.

Silver is widely distributed in nature, but the total amount is quite small. It is normally recovered during the processing of **lead**, **copper**, and **zinc** ores.

Sodium (Na)

Element 11 on the **periodic table**. A soft, silvery-white **metal** of **group 1** (the **alkali metals**).

It is a common element, especially as the **compound** sodium chloride—common salt.

Sodium is the most common alkali metal and the sixth most abundant element on Earth. Sodium metal is very **reactive**. It easily ignites in air and reacts vigorously with water to release **hydrogen**, which then catches fire.

Sodium is widely used to make chemicals and also for yellow sodium vapor bulbs.

▲ **Silver**—Silver is extremely reflective and is used for mirrors.

Soluble

The property of **dissolving** in a liquid. The dissolving liquid is called the **solvent**. (*Compare with:* **Insoluble**.)

Solute

A substance that has **dissolved** in a **solution**.

Solution

A mixture containing one substance **dissolved** in a **solvent**.

Solvent

The main substance in a **solution**.

Strontium (Sr)

Element 38 on the **periodic table**. A soft, leadlike **metal** of **group 2** (the **alkaline earths**).

It was discovered in 1790 by the Scottish scientists Adair Crawford and William Cruikshank.

Strontium has few uses except as the red color in signal flares. **Radioactive isotopes** of strontium are produced during nuclear explosions, and they are the main health hazard in radioactive fallout.

Sodium pellet

◄ **Sodium**—Sodium is a soft, silvery-looking metal that tarnishes very quickly. Here a clear face has just been cut with a spatula. The sodium is being held with tongs.

Sulfur (S)

Element 16 on the **periodic table**. A yellow **nonmetal** in **group 6** (the **oxygen group**).

It is one of the most **reactive** of the elements. It is the ninth most abundant element in the universe and is the third most common element in **minerals** after **oxygen** and **silicon**.

Pure sulfur is a brittle solid that is a poor conductor of electricity and is **insoluble** in water.

Sulfur has been known since ancient times as brimstone.

▼ **Strontium**—Strontium produces a distinctive red flame when burned.

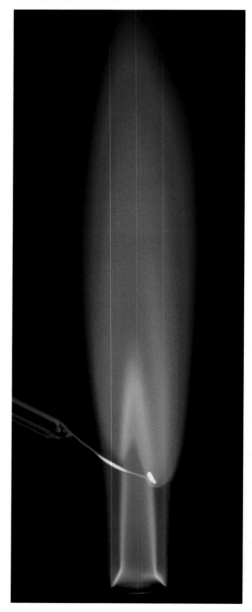

▼ **Sulfur**—Sulfur forms golden crystals.

Technetium (Tc)

Element 43 on the **periodic table**. An artificial **radioactive**, silvery **metal** that belongs to the **transition metals**.

It was the first element to be artificially produced in 1937 by Carlo Perrier and Emilio Segrè. It is used as a fuel in nuclear reactors.

Tellurium (Te)

Element 52 on the **periodic table**. A silvery-white **metalloid** in **group 6** (the **oxygen group**).

It was discovered in 1782 by Franz Joseph Müller von Reichenstein.

A poor conductor of heat and a moderate conductor of electricity, it has not been widely used.

Terbium (Tb)

Element 65 on the **periodic table**. A silvery-white **metal** belonging to the **rare-earth metals** and one of the **lanthanides**.

It was discovered in 1843 by Carl Gustaf Mosander. It has few uses.

Thallium (Tl)

Element 81 on the **periodic table**. A blue-gray leadlike **metal** that is part of **group 3** (the **boron group**).

It was discovered in 1861 by Sir William Crookes. Thallium has no uses.

T

Tantalum (Ta)

Element 73 on the **periodic table**. This rare, very hard, silver-gray **metal** is one of the **transition metals**.

It is very dense and has a high melting point. It was discovered in 1802 by the Swedish chemist Anders Gustaf Ekeberg and named after the mythological character Tantalus. Its main use is in **corrosion**-resistant containers and in electrical components called capacitors.

Tarnish

A coating that develops as a result of a **reaction** between a **metal** and substances in the air. Most commonly, tarnishing forms an **oxide**.

▼ **Tarnish**—Tarnishing over time can be seen with these three dated coins.

Thorium (Th)

Element 90 on the **periodic table**. A silvery-white **radioactive metal** of the **actinide series**.

It was discovered in 1828 by Jöns Jacob Berzelius. Thorium is added to **magnesium alloys** to improve their high-temperature strength.

Thulium (Tm)

Element 69 on the **periodic table**. A **rare-earth metal** and one of the **lanthanides**.

Thulium was discovered in 1879 by Per Teodor Cleve, who named it after an ancient word for Scandinavia. It is particularly rare and has few uses.

Titanium (Ti)

Element 22 on the **periodic table**. A silvery-gray **metal** belonging to the **transition metals**.

It has a low density and great strength and also resists **corrosion** well. It was discovered in 1791 by the English chemist William Gregor. **Alloyed** with other metals, it is used for replacement hips and in aircraft.

Tin (Sn)

Element 50 on the **periodic table**. A soft, silvery-white **metal** of **group 4** (the **carbon group**). It has been known since earliest times, when it was alloyed with **copper** to make **bronze**. Tin is highly resistant to **corrosion** because, on exposure to air, it forms a thin film of tin **oxide** on its surface. Tin is easily worked (**malleable**) and has a low melting point.

▲ **Tin**—Because tin is unreactive, it has been used extensively in the canning industry to coat steel cans. In this picture you can see how the can rusts if the tin is scraped off and the steel exposed to the air.

It has been used for protecting steel in cans and on cooking dishes.

Tin is a weak metal and is not used for any form of construction. **Alloys** that include tin are solder, pewter, bronze, and bell metal.

Transition elements, transition metals

Broadly defined as those **elements** in the middle of the **periodic table** between **groups 2** and **3**. They are all **metals** and make up the majority of the known elements, including the **lanthanides (rare-earth metals)** and **actinides**.

The members of the transition metals are as follows, in ascending atomic number (those which are more commonly found are shown in bold italics): **scandium**, *titanium*, *vanadium*, *chromium*, *manganese*, *iron*, *cobalt*, *nickel*, *copper*, *zinc*, **yttrium**, *zirconium*, **niobium**, *molybdenum*, **technetium**, **ruthenium**, **rhodium**, **palladium**, *silver*, *cadmium*, **lutetium**, **hafnium**, *tantalum*, *tungsten*, **rhenium**, **osmium**, **iridium**, *platinum*, *gold*, *mercury*, **lawrencium**, **rutherfordium**, **dubnium**, **seaborgium**, **bohrium**, **hassium**, **meitnerium**, **ununnilium**, **unununium**, and **ununbium**.

In addition, there are groups of very rare elements that make up part of the transition metals. These elements are part of the lanthanide and actinide series of metals and are shown on the periodic table at the bottom.

The lanthanide metals are, in ascending atomic number order: **lanthanium**, **cerium**, **praseodymium**, **neodymium**, **promethium**, **samarium**, **europium**, **gadolinium**, **terbium**, **dysprosium**, **holmium**, **erbium**, **thulium**, and **ytterbium**.

The actinide metals are, in ascending atomic number order: **actinium**, **thorium**, **protactinium**, *uranium*, **neptunium**, *plutonium*, **americium**, **curium**, **berkelium**, **californium**, **einsteinium**, **fermium**, **mendelevium**, and **nobelium**.

Properties

The transition elements are all metals and have the following general properties:

▶ They have one or two **electrons** in their outer **shells**.

▶ They are all hard and strong, with high densities, high melting points, and high boiling points.

▶ They form a number of oxidation states (for example, iron(II) and iron(III)).

▶ They tend to form colored **compounds** (for example, iron(II) compounds are often green, and iron(III) compounds are often orange-brown).

▶ Many are **catalysts** (for example, vanadium and manganese).

▶ Many are good conductors of heat and electricity (for example, silver and copper).

▶ Many can easily be bent (are **malleable**)–they are easily beaten into sheets or drawn into wires, for example, iron.

▶ They all form basic **oxides** (but some can also react with both alkalis and acids—for example, zinc and manganese(VII) oxide).

▶ Most of them quickly develop a protective oxide coating when exposed to air, and most are fairly unreactive (for example, gold).

▶ When they react, they tend to lose electrons, forming positive **ions**—**cations** (for example, Fe^{2+} and Mn^{2+}).

Transuranium elements

Elements that have **atomic numbers** greater than 92 on the **periodic table**; thus they all lie beyond **uranium**.

Tungsten (W)

Element 74 on the **periodic table**. A white to grayish **metal** belonging to the **transition metals**. Tungsten is also called wolfram.

It is the strongest metal in existence and has the highest melting point. It was discovered in 1783 by the Spanish chemists Juan José and Fausto Elhuyar. It is used as an **alloy** with steel and in the filaments of bulbs. As tungsten carbide, it is used for drill bits.

U

Ununbium (Uub)

Element 112 on the **periodic table**. One of the most recently discovered elements, very little is so far known about it. Only a few **atoms** of it have ever been made. That was done by fusing a **zinc** atom with a **lead** atom using a heavy **ion** accelerator. Atoms of this element have a lifespan of less than a millisecond.

Element 112 was discovered in 1996 by S. Hofmann, V. Ninov, F. P. Hessberger, P. Armbruster, H. Folger, G. Münzenberg, and others at Darmstadt, Germany.

Ununhexium (Uuh)

Element 116 on the **periodic table**. One of the most recently discovered elements, only a few **atoms** have ever been made. They were as a result of the decay of **ununoctium**. Ununoctium decays less than a millisecond after its formation to make element 116, which then decays in a similarly short time.

Ununnilium (Uun)

Element 110 on the **periodic table**. One of the most recently discovered elements, only a few **atoms** have ever been made. Its properties are probably similar to those of platinum, except that ununnilium is unstable and decays in a millisecond.

Many billions of **nickel** atoms were fired at a **lead** target in order to produce a single atom of ununnilium.

Ununoctium (Uuo)

Element 118 on the **periodic table**. One of the most recently discovered elements, only a few **atoms** have ever been made. The experiment was carried out using calculations by Robert Smolanczuk (Soltan Institute for Nuclear Studies, Poland) on the **fusion** of atomic nuclei.

The atoms were produced by fusing a **krypton**-86 **ion** with **lead**-208 atom using an accelerator. It took 11 days to produce 3 atoms, which then decomposed in a millisecond to **ununhexium**.

Ununquadium (Uuq)

Element 114 on the **periodic table**. One of the most recently discovered elements, only a few **atoms** have ever been made. These atoms were produced by nuclear **fusion** of a **calcium** atom with a **plutonium** atom.

It was discovered by workers at the Nuclear Institute at Dubna, Russia, in December 1998.

Unununium (Uuu)

Element 111 on the **periodic table**. One of the most recently discovered elements, only a few **atoms** have ever been made. That involved the nuclear **fusion** of an **isotope** of **bismuth** with an isotope of **nickel** using a heavy **ion** accelerator.

Unununium was discovered on December 8, 1994, at Darmstadt in Germany by S. Hofmann, V. Ninov, F. P. Hessberger, P. Armbruster, H. Folger, G. Münzenberg, and others.

Uranium (U)

Element 92 on the **periodic table**. The best known **radioactive** element in the **actinide series**. Uranium is found naturally.

Uranium is a dense, hard, silvery-white **metal** that can easily be shaped (**malleable**). It was discovered in 1789 by Martin Heinrich Klaproth and named after the planet Uranus. However, it was not until 1896 that the French physicist Henri Becquerel discovered that uranium was radioactive. During the 1930s it was realized that uranium could be bombarded by slow **neutrons** to cause a chain reaction leading to a nuclear explosion. This is the basis of the atomic bomb.

Its main use is as a nuclear fuel. One kilogram of uranium produces the same energy as three million kilograms of coal.

(*See also:* **Actinium** and **Fission**.)

▲ **Uranium**—A piece of uranium from a nuclear reactor.

V

Valency

The number of **bonds** that an **atom** can form.

For example, **calcium** has a valency of two, and **bromine** a valency of one.

Vanadium (V)

Element 23 on the **periodic table**. A silvery-white soft **metal** belonging to the **transition metals**.

It was discovered in 1801 by the Spanish mineralogist Andrés Manuel del Río. It was named after the Scandinavian goddess of beauty and youth, Vana. This was suggested by the range of beautiful colors that are produced by vanadium **compounds**.

It can be **alloyed** with steel to make strong drill bits.

X

Xenon (Xe)

Element 54 on the **periodic table**. One of the **group 8** elements (**noble gases**).

It is a very rare, heavy gas that is colorless, odorless, and tasteless. It was discovered in 1898 by the British chemists Sir William Ramsay and Morris W. Travers.

Xenon is unreactive. When electricity passes through it, xenon emits a bluish light.

▼ **Vanadium**—Vanadium is well known for its colorful compounds.

Y

Ytterbium (Yb)

Element 70 on the **periodic table**. A **metal** belonging to the **rare-earth metals** and one of the **lanthanides**.

Discovered in 1878 by Jean-Charles-Galinard de Marignac. He named it after the town of Ytterby, Sweden, where the rocks are unusually rich in rare earths. It has few uses.

Yttrium (Y)

Element 39 on the **periodic table**. A silvery **metal** belonging to the **rare-earth metals** and one of the **lanthanides**.

Discovered in 1794 by Johan Gadolin and named after the town Ytterby, Sweden, where the rocks are unusually rich in rare earths.

Yttrium is used in metal **alloys** and for the red dots (phosphors) on color television tubes.

Z

Zinc (Zn)

Element 30 on the **periodic table**. A soft, easily shaped, gray **metal** belonging to the **transition metals**.

A commonly used metal, zinc has been **alloyed** with **copper** to produce **brass** for thousands of years. Zinc is an essential trace **mineral** in the human body. It **corrodes** slowly and is used as a protective coating on steel; the combination is called galvanized iron.

Zirconium (Zr)

Element 40 on the **periodic table**. A soft, white **metal** belonging to the **transition metals**.

Zirconium was discovered in 1824 by the Swedish chemist Jöns Jacob Berzelius. Crystals of zirconium **oxide** are used in jewelry as a substitute for diamond, where it is known as cubic zirconia. It is also used as a structural material in nuclear reactors and as an **alloy** with **magnesium** and steel.

▲ **Zirconium**—Zirconium oxide makes common artificial diamonds.

Sphalerite

▲ **Zinc**—Zinc sulfide, sphalerite, is the main ore of zinc. It is shown here as the dark brown crystals together with yellow cubes of pyrite and some colorless quartz crystals.

▶ **Zinc**—Zinc is used to protect other metals through galvanizing. The steel rods holding up the Brooklyn Bridge are galvanized (zinc-coated) steel.

Index